Reflections: The Student View

Using Hindsight For Foresight

Callum Lawson-Gallagher, Ravi Gollapalli & Johnny Sheridan

Cover designed by: Nour Hajjar

ISBN-13: 9798847664288

Imprint: Independently published

This book contains the perspectives of over 100 college students who reflect on the highs and lows of university life.

You don't have to read the book like you would read a novel, research paper or autobiography.

Do what feels natural to you.

If you aren't sure where to start, pick any topic from the book, engage with the question, consider the reflections, and encourage your curiosity to run wild.

"Coping with loneliness is something that isn't taught to us in school. It is something that many of us experience, especially when we reach third level. First year of college can often depict itself as this thrilling adventure where expectations of success, independence, or new relationships prevail. But often, the transition from school can be daunting. Sometimes we feel isolated. We see our choices but don't know how to make the right one. How can we be resilient? How can we feel liberated from these so-called norms that we are supposedly expected to rise to? This book provides tender insights into the lives of those who have experienced the highs and lows of being a college student. Through their experiences, we draw solace from learning from others' reflections which shows us resilience in action and helps us to figure out our own pace when it comes to navigating this new chapter in our lives."

- Adam McNally, Former Nightline Executive & Current Masters Student in the University of Utrecht

Acknowledgements

Reflections: The Student View is the product of three very different but like-minded graduates, over 100 anonymous contributors, and other individuals who aided us in self-publishing a book. Without contributors, there would be no book. These reflections are collective convictions, experiences, intuitions, and memories of students who have experienced their university years in different times and places around the world. We are so grateful to everyone who contributed. And also toward those who helped us with a wide array of problems.

Our gratitude extends particularly to Nour Hajjar. Nour helped us tremendously with design and was invaluable - both as a friend and designer - until completion. Additionally, we would like to thank Gloria Zapata. Gloria helped us hugely regarding advisory and execution. We want to thank our parents, our university, our family and friends for encouraging us to channel our curiosity, providing us with the opportunity to work freely and pushing us to pursue the areas of life where we feel a sense of passion. Although we had the initiative to ask our peers and friends for their reflections, we are not saviours, rescuers, or prophets. From our perspective, this book isn't about us. It's about sharing the reflections of a diverse group of people and helping others get what they want out of life.

Thank You.

Contents

Reflections: The Student View

About Reflections: The Student View

On the Southern slopes of South Africa's Helderberg mountain sits a 980-acre Nature Reserve. Much of the reserve consists of a species-rich vegetation type, with over 700 different species calling it home. For life to prosper, the nature reserve must survive a ferocious fire season in the Western Cape. Fires can begin via wind, lightning or falling rocks but more commonly occur by accident, caused by humans, indifferent to the consequences of their carelessness.

And yet, despite a fire season occurring every year, the reserve and its wildlife survive. The secret? Controlled burn. When necessary, The City of Cape Town employs competent firefighters to prescribe a burn to protect vulnerable species, allowing the reserve to rejuvenate and flourish.

Although forest fires are a matter of interest, the passage above solely serves as a metaphor. This book investigates prescribed psychological fires that encourage growth. We focus specifically on reflections from past and present university students. **We believe in using hindsight for foresight**, hoping history allows one to anticipate future events and experiences.

By embracing this book, you can:
- ❖ **Remember** where you were
- ❖ **Take Action** from where you are
- ❖ **Manifest** where you are heading

As a trio, **we don't know anything.** This book is the result of adopting a position of humility, being open with one another and accepting that we are all still learning. To help make the experience of reading this book more valuable, we recommend you ponder the same questions we asked our contributors. We hope that our work and the reflections of our contributors will lead you to **discover valuable reflections.**

THE PAST

The Past encourages us to **Remember**.

Remember where you were. We cover short summaries of university years, bright and bleak misconceptions, risky decisions, delayed habits, and nostalgia-inducing memories. This chapter ends with insights into practical principles which, in hindsight, would have provided value to students across their university journey.

The following is the Student View of **The Past**.

Write a sentence that summarizes your time at university.

❖ A beginning of a journey to understand who I am and who I want to become.

❖ The more you give, the more you get. Coming into university I was a bit apprehensive to socialise and try and make new friends as I was quite reserved and shy my whole life. But I told myself, if not now, when? I wanted to network and get to know new people. A principle that I hold very closely is that of inclusiveness. I believe including others is vital to a well-connected and enjoyable experience of any sort. But if you aren't willing to go through such lengths to put yourself out there, don't expect great things in return.

❖ I'd describe my time at university to be similar to that of 'bumper cars' at a Fair. You'd have many bumps along the way and at first it was a big shock, but you got used to it after a while as you knew how to manoeuvre the car better and the bumps didn't seem so bad which is when the experience became fun.

❖ During my first week of uni, I dreamt that I let the current take me, instead of trying to fight it. I didn't know where the current was taking me, but I could feel that it was the right way.

❖ My university years have been intense concerning study, exciting regarding meeting new people and fulfilling when it comes to part-time jobs I've done.

❖ Stepping out of my comfort zone into the real world.

❖ You learn to spread your wings socially, gaining more confidence as you mature.

❖ A time of huge development personally, socially, and professionally that has changed where my life is set to go next.

Write a sentence that summarizes your time at university.

- ❖ You can do anything, but not everything.

- ❖ Challenging and frustrating but valuable.

- ❖ University has been transformative; it has shown me that hard work can be fun if you are surrounded by the right people.

- ❖ Constant growth, reflection and getting to know myself better.

- ❖ University is the springboard that launches the trajectory of the rest of your adult life, socially, professionally and spiritually. Which direction you take, how far you get and how fast you go is completely up to you.

- ❖ Awakening to the incompetence of the world.

- ❖ When we hit our lowest point, we are open to our greatest change.

- ❖ It's not about the academics, the people make it worthwhile.

- ❖ Lots of wasted time.

- ❖ I spent two years wondering what it was that I ought to be doing; one year doing it without realising as much, and a fourth year recognising this, and hoping that I was right.

- ❖ Embracing the freedom to discover my true self and learning to love her unconditionally.

- ❖ A life changing experience where I not only got to network with some fantastic people but also create a better version of myself. Wouldn't change a thing.

- ❖ The trials and tribulations of balancing all aspects of life.

- ❖ University has been a delightfully expansive and challenging experience which has bent my brain into new shapes and inspired (and overwhelmed) me in its embodiment of incredible human potential and bountiful possibility.

❖ Once I got into the rhythm of college, post secondary school, I could finally be my true self and no longer be silently judged.

❖ I didn't make the most of it and I wish I went at an older age.

❖ The first time I have had to struggle to balance my social life, my study, and a part time job, but a fun struggle.

❖ A grinding show of tenacity and endurance.

❖ Don't be sad because it's over, be happy because it happened.

❖ It was one of the most incredibly difficult but rewarding, perspective-shifting, relationship building times of my life.

❖ High highs and low lows, but the friends I've made here keep me going.

❖ I attended for 2 years on a 3-year BA program abroad from the states, and then dropped out.

❖ I started out feeling lost, and I'm still finding where I'm going.

❖ My experience of university in Ireland is one of mixed emotion as I experienced very narrow-minded lecturers which ultimately discouraged me from an area that I thought I would love, versus a group of lecturers that were supportive and enthusiastic, triggering me to pursue a career in the sector.

❖ An attempt to learn under the same, normal system during unstable and irregular times.

❖ Learned to be a grown-up which included managing time (especially when there's such little free time), money, relationships and just how to navigate life making the past few years a huge learning experience.

❖ Juggling social health, mental health, physical health and performing accordingly.

❖ Uncertainty is certain. Better be certain about your habits and learning.

❖ College years are all about LEARNING… and not only about your course, but about yourself!!

❖ A discordant mixture of faces, papers, and distant memories, punctuated by lucid, vivid, and jubilant memories.

❖ It was a memorable four years where I made lifelong friends but I do wish I pushed myself a little harder to get involved more and to not be afraid of doing things alone.

❖ A rollercoaster that felt like it lasted only a few seconds.

❖ My time at university was enjoyable, I made amazing friends and evolved as a person. My view of the world and human nature have matured. I now feel like I have my own identity.

❖ Stuck in between the reality and the internet.

❖ Learned so much more than what my course provided. Was dealt challenges. Succeeded against some. Failed against others. Learned to learn from both. Seized the small things when they came.

❖ Both very tiring and very exhilarating at the same time.

❖ University is a metric that assists many to understand what they truly want to learn and pursue in life.

❖ Start, stop, start again, thanks Covid.

❖ You will never have enough sleep.

❖ Half online, half in person, never got the full experience.

❖ A fresh start that became a transformative time.

❖ University has been one fantastic disaster after another.

❖ College is an experience where you attempt to become an adult in your own way while being pushed in ways that are the conventional ones.

❖ My time at university was the most challenging, rewarding and eye-opening experience of my life, so far.

❖ A cocktail of new experiences, friendships, and laughter with a sprinkle of education.

❖ Inconsistent.

❖ A time for spreading wings & next-morning head pings.

❖ Making memories with new people along with learning valuable life skills.

❖ The best, hardest, craziest, fulfilling, tiring years of my life.

❖ A stressful and at times soul-rending experience that I would do all over again if given the chance.

❖ A socially driven experience with a bit of study and hardship on the side.

❖ If you regularly do what you've regularly done, you'll receive what you've regularly received, so choose what you do wisely.

❖ It's my second home, where I truly figured myself out.

❖ An incredible time to meet amazing people.

❖ The only constant is change.

❖ Extremely worthwhile, probably learnt more from the personal side of it than the academic side of university.

❖ Challenges are merely half as difficult as the path taken to get to it.

❖ My initial college experiences were robust and exciting in my first two years, becoming uneventful in the middle (as I stared aimlessly at Zoom throughout the pandemic), finally finishing in 2022 amidst a cacophony of exams, assignments, and job searching!

Write a sentence that summarizes your time at university.

- ❖ The time spent with new friends was always time well spent.

- ❖ Four years of variety from psychology to management, undergrad to postgrad, stress inducing to stress relieving, all encompassed by inspiring openness and tremendous diversity.

- ❖ An intriguing and stimulating environment, where I've learned a lot about myself and made friends for life.

- ❖ A worthwhile experience which taught me patience and resilience in the face of challenges and adversity.

- ❖ You get out of it what you put into it.

- ❖ Waste of f*cking time while in lectures but great any other times.

- ❖ "I feel rotten after yesterday."

- ❖ Almost didn't make it sane.

- ❖ It was all going really well until suddenly it really wasn't.

- ❖ A tightrope crossed with adequate balance.

- ❖ You can do anything, but not everything, just don't do nothing!

- ❖ My time at university was very rewarding, from friendship, character building, knowledge to self-development.

- ❖ It has been an enjoyable experience, however it has included many setbacks along the way due to Covid.

- ❖ Time to grow.

- ❖ An educational journey with lack of purpose.

- ❖ Humbling, enjoyable, painful, prideful.

- ❖ Information and sensory overload.

❖ I chose to study the "safe option" and learnt what I don't want to spend the rest of my life doing - it was the time that I had outside of Uni that opened my eyes to what makes me come alive.

❖ A time to connect with people.

❖ University for me was like Bitcoin. It had its peaks, which made me on top of the world. It had its troughs, which at times induced a lot stress and anxiety. But overall, despite the volatility of emotions, my experience was positive.

❖ Tough times never last, only tough people last.

❖ "Can all students please mute themselves during the online lecture."

What is the greatest misconception you had before attending university?

- ❖ I would know what I'm doing when I leave.

- ❖ That lecturers were as strict and unapproachable as the teachers in Secondary School. Nobody will rip my head off for asking for an extension and most lectures are really friendly.

- ❖ That I would make loads of friends. In reality, it can be pretty challenging to make new friends when you are in very large courses.

- ❖ Adults knew what they were doing.

- ❖ That it would be hard to make new friends.

- ❖ That it would be harder than school was. Turns out nothing in life can be harder than secondary school.

- ❖ University is all about nights-out.

- ❖ That there would be loads of activities and events to socialise on my campus.

- ❖ College is all about studying.

- ❖ That everyone else has their sh*t figured out.

- ❖ That there is only ever one truth.

- ❖ University is the answer to success and more importantly, to learning.

- ❖ That I would know what I wanted to do afterwards.

- ❖ That it would be like in the movies, with lots of parties and travels.

- ❖ That it would be easy.

❖ That I'd have a lot of spare time for myself. I always felt like there was something that I had to be doing, I never rested.

❖ I should care what random people think about me.

❖ That it will be so difficult that you can't keep up with hobbies and sports.

❖ Degree = career, as in you don't have to follow the normal career your degree hints towards, it's really fluid and many places don't care about which degree you do.

❖ That my sports career would take off from playing through college. I didn't have enough motivation or discipline to execute that. I did end up taking other unexpected routes of life.

❖ That college is hard work to understand or grasp, it's not, it's just putting time in.

❖ That I would feel more grown up and have greater insight into what I want to do with my life.

❖ You will no longer be held down.

❖ That my greatest times would be in school, times in college were much more valuable and more testing to me.

❖ College is a party 24/7.

❖ That it was like secondary school.

❖ As an international student, that it would be quick & easy to make friends with locals. In First Year, my peers stuck to the people they knew. Branch out! There's so many cool & different people out there to learn from.

❖ That everyone cares about you and how you dress/act.

Recall a risky decision or venture, what did you learn?

❖ I co-founded a startup in my 3rd year of university with a married couple in their late thirties. The start up eventually failed a few months later and I learnt so much over that time, but the most crucial lessons were:

1. Coming into a job/startup as a student with no experience can make you feel like you have no value to add and as a result you may be tempted to play your value down - don't do that. Own your value and don't work for free!

2. You have to be 100% certain about your business partners - if you get a bad feeling about your partners, walk away early. You can't build a great business with the wrong people.

❖ I was on a placement in Germany doing Event Management, in Berlin. I fell off an E-Scooter after a night out and almost died. I was in a coma for 11 days, & in the hospital for about a month and a half. My family was distraught & came to visit me not knowing if they'd see me conscious ever again… But I'm on top of the world now (: it's changed my perspective on how careful you have to be when you're drinking & especially when you're abroad, & how important head protection is.

❖ Flying to Brazil by myself at age 20 without speaking a word of Portuguese. It was my very first overseas trip without my parents. It taught me resilience and how to fend for myself. It was not an easy trip with many ups and downs. It also made me appreciate how lucky I am to have grown up in New Zealand.

❖ After finishing my Masters abroad, I had to make a difficult decision: Whether to go back to the motherland or stay abroad and try to get a job there. The easiest thing to do was to go back home: I wouldn't need to pay rent and I wouldn't struggle with the language. However, I told myself that if I went back home and get a job there, I would probably never leave… so I took a risk and stayed abroad. The first 6 months were really tough. I couldn't get a job in my field so I had 2 part-time jobs to be able to pay for food & rent. At the same time, I was actively looking for a proper job which meant I had to spend a lot of time preparing and doing interviews. I did dozens of them! Some went really well, others really bad. I only needed 1 offer, 1 opportunity, and after what it seemed like an eternity… I got it! Now I have a job I love and my career is developing as well as it possibly could!

❖ Deciding to backpack for 7 months - I learned that I don't need to follow the traditional path pushed on me by my university.

❖ Last minute assignment writing. The usual. Still not really learning from it. I might like the rush and adrenaline it gives knowing you don't have much time left.

❖ Quitting my job to focus on college - I learned that money disappears when you spend it.

❖ Not going back for my 4th year. It reminded me how much fun uni really was. It also taught me that uni is quite inefficient and you can teach yourself an amazing amount if you are dedicated enough.

❖ Investing in Rheinmetall in 2021, I learned that arms manufacturing is lucrative yet it is something that doesn't sit well with my sense of morality.

❖ Arriving in a new city for a year of study abroad with no accommodation. Learned that things usually work out eventually, always stay positive and seek out help from others.

❖ A risky decision I made was to get involved with a venture that was out of my comfort zone and had no strong correlation to what I studied. I was questioned by people in my course and even college career counsellors as to why I'm putting so much time into something that isn't related to my degree, but the learning and growth I got out of it was immense. The hardest part was escaping imposter syndrome, and once I started backing myself, I began seeing much more positive results in my work.

❖ Going travelling on my own for the first time in the summer before First Year. I learned that if you put yourself out there & be open to anything, you'll experience and learn much more than you would if you had confined yourself.

❖ Investing in the Cryptocurrency world. Extremely risky if you do not know what you are doing, but this has taught me patience and discipline.

❖ In May 2020, I had to make a very difficult and risky decision about whether or not I would return home from campus to be with family during the national lockdown, or whether I would remain on campus. I decided to remain on campus in order to make use of the resources and facilities in my residence in order to complete academic obligations. I ran the risk of not seeing my family for months, but it paid off. Naturally, my family was upset, and did not understand. But I was willing to bet on myself. It taught me to make the necessary sacrifices, even when others do not share or see the vision.

❖ Deciding to go to university. I learned that I wasn't ready at that moment, but that didn't mean that I couldn't try again.

❖ What you think may be difficult/risky is actually easier than you think. You can always achieve a lot more than you initially believe.

What one habit do you wish you had developed earlier?

❖ Making learning people's names a priority when you meet new people.

❖ Better discipline/focus. While I always submitted assignments on time and engaged appropriately with the course material I had in university, it was often completed at the expense of my own well-being. I would severely procrastinate and leave things until the very last minute. Had I developed a system to better coordinate what I needed to get done, maybe there wouldn't have been so much undue stress and pressure.

❖ Writing summarising papers with key information for exams. I have discovered it is really helpful for me.

❖ Talking to strangers.

❖ Disagreeing to do something I don't want to do.

❖ The courage to be bold.

❖ Giving less of a fu*k what people think about you.

❖ Sleeping and waking up at consistent times every day.

❖ Cold showers.

❖ Confidence in engagement with my superiors.

❖ Patience.

❖ Coding for fun in my free time.

❖ I wish I had started using Google calendar earlier.

❖ Keeping a diary, I don't write in it every day, however it is nice to look back on my past emotions, thoughts and feelings. If you ever feel down, looking back at old experiences in your diary can be really helpful. It is also rewarding to see how far you have come.

❖ Meditating.

❖ Helping others more.

❖ Managing my tasks better (e.g. ordering by priority and assigning time to them).

❖ Budgeting.

❖ Including in my daily routine some physical activities (even just a walk).

❖ Eating healthy.

❖ Being more proactive about taking charge in life (whether that be for personal pursuits or academic endeavours).

❖ Allocating ~one hour everyday to read the Financial Times.

❖ The ability to appreciate time off/holidays.

❖ A healthy sleep schedule.

❖ Exercising consistently.

❖ Starting to work on my essays earlier and referencing correctly.

❖ Drinking more water.

❖ Getting up early.

❖ Mindfulness.

❖ Prioritising a better work-life balance. It is very overwhelming at university for some people that have immense pressure on themselves. I was one of them. You assume you need to work yourself to the point of burnout to make it through. Having outstanding results is not always great, there is no guarantee you will secure employment based on that, having experienced it first-hand.

❖ What you will cherish forever are the experiences you allowed yourself to partake in. Remember to take time along the way to smell the roses as well.

❖ Writing down what needs to be done, and by when.

❖ Wake up early and be productive.

❖ To read everyday for at least 1 hour.

❖ Planning ahead and time management.

❖ Seeing friends during the week instead of overworking myself, balance is key.

❖ Running for my sanity.

❖ Putting myself out there as often as possible (still not quite there).

❖ Being selfish with my time and managing it according to my needs.

❖ Getting things done right away that take less than 2 minutes.

❖ Two twenty-minute Transcendental Meditation sessions every day.

❖ A good work ethic, mainly at the start of projects, would have been handy if I worked harder at the start.

Meaningful Highlights

Throughout this book, we feature four different "Meaningful Highlights". For example, Meaningful Highlight 1 encouraged contributors to name a song that is meaningful to them. Other highlights are featured throughout the book.

Meaningful Highlight 1
You can understand someone's heart by the music they like.

Angel - Massive Attack

Asilazi - Johnny Clegg

Bella Ciao - the 19th Century 'mondine'

Big Ships - e-dubble

Bitter Sweet Symphony - The Verve

Brake - Infinite Bisous

Californication - Red Hot Chili Peppers

Cardiac Arrest - Bad Suns

Castle On the Hill - Ed Sheeran

Clare to Here - The Fureys & Davey Arthur

Clay Pigeons - Blaze Foley

Comptine d'un Autre été, l'après-midi - Yann Tiersen

Cross My Mind - ARIZONA

Daddy Cool - Boney M

Dancing in the Moonlight - Thin Lizzie

Danny Boy - Johnny Cash

Dil Dhadakne Do -Shankar Mahadevan

Disco Inferno - 50 Cent

DNA. - Kendrick Lamar

Do You Hear the People Sing? - Les Miserables Original Cast

Don't Worry, Be Happy - Bobby McFerrin

Doo Be Doo - Freshlyground

Dosed - Red Hot Chili Peppers

Dreamer - Supertramp

Exchange - Bryson Tiller

You can understand someone's heart by the music they like.

Famous - Kanye West

Father & Friend - Alain Clark

Father and Son - Cat Stevens

Feed On Greed - The Undercover Hippy

Feeling Good - Nina Simone

Fireball - Pitbull

Firework - Katy Perry

Five Years - David Bowie

Fix You - Coldplay

Folsom Prison Blues - Johnny Cash

From Clare to Here - Ralph McTell

Glasgow - Catfish & the Bottlemen

Go Solo - Zwette (feat. Tom Rosenthal)

Haven't Met You Yet - Michael Bublé

Here Comes the Hotstepper - Ini Kamoze

Holocene - Bon Iver

Human - Rag'n'Bone Man

Human Beings - Seal

Human Sadness - The Voidz

Hunnybee - Unknown Metal Orchestra

I Know Who I Am - Sinach

I Lied - Lord Huron

I Like to Move It - Will.i.am

If I Could - Jazz

If I Would Have Known - Kyle Hume

I'm On Fire - Bruce Springsteen

Imagine - John Lennon

It's Only Sex - Car Seat Headrest

Jamming - Bob Marley

Just Do You - Lord Echo

Keep Your Head Up - Ben Howard

King - Florence + the Machine

Reflections

You can understand someone's heart by the music they like.

Lean On Me - Bill Withers

Lose Yourself - Eminem

Lost - Frank Ocean

Love Yours - J Cole

Martxa Baten Lehen Notak - Mikel Laboa

Memory Lane - Nas

Midnight Train – Jazz Sheridan

Miles Away - Years Around the Sun

Million Questions - Patrick Jørgensen

Mise Éire - Patrick Cassidy (feat. Sibéal)

Montaña - Gipsy Kings

Moving - Bugzy Malone

Mr. Brightside - The Killers

Neon - John Mayer

Never Gonna Give You Up - Rick Astley

Not Nineteen Forever - Courteneers

One Day - Matisyahu

One Way Ticket - Eruption

Over the Rainbow - Israel Kamakawiwo'ole

Paris - The 1975

Pata Pata - Miriam Makeba

Peer Gynt Suite No. 1, Op. 46: 1. Morning Mood - London Philharmonic Orchestra & David Parry

Piyaar Sufiyana - Farhan Saeed & Asim Jofa

Piano Man - Billy Joel

Poetic Justice - Kendrick Lamar

PRIDE. - Kendrick Lamar

Raglan Road - The Dubliners

Reborn - KIDS SEE GHOSTS

Redemption Song - Bob Marley & the Wailers

Rock 'N' Roll Kids - Brendan Shine

Runaway - Kanye West

You can understand someone's heart by the music they like.

Rushing Water - Sting

Shampoo Bottles - Peach Pit

(Sittin' On) The Dock of the Bay - Otis Redding

Slipping Through My Fingers - ABBA

Slomo - Slowdive

Somebody I Used to Know - Gotye

Soundtrack 2 My Life - Kid Cudi

Spirit Bird - Xavier Rudd

State Lines - Novo Amor

Stay Positive - The Streets

Stolen Dance - Milky Chance

Streets of Philadelphia - Bruce Springsteen

Sweet Disposition - The Temper Trap

Take My Hand - Picture This

Talkin' Bout a Revolution - Tracy Chapman

The Boy with the Arab Strap - Belle & Sebastian

The Cult of Dionysus - The Orion Experience

The Fields of Athenry - The Dubliners

The Lowlands of Holland - The Levellers

The Masterplan - Oasis

The Scientist - Coldplay

The Stolen Child - The Waterboys

There Will Be Time - Mumford & Sons

These Streets - Paolo Nutini

This is Not a Song, It's an Outburst - Rodriguez

This Must Be the Place - Talking Heads

This Night Has Opened My Eyes - The Smiths

Through the Wire - Kanye West

Todo De Tí - Rauw Alejandro

Toes - Glass Animals

Too Late to Turn Back Now - Cornelius Brothers & Sister Rose

Vienna - Billy Joel

Reflections

You can understand someone's heart by the music they like.

Visiting Hours - Ed Sheeran

Waitin' On a Sunny Day - Bruce Springsteen

Waka Waka - Shakira & Freshlyground

Way Back Home - Salvatore Ganacci

Way It Goes - Hippo Campus

What A Wonderful World - Louis Armstrong

What They Want - Russ

Wing$ - Macklemore & Ryan Lewis

Wonderwall - Oasis

Worry - Jack Garratt

You Only Live Once - The Strokes

You've Got a Friend - James Taylor

Which day from your time at university would you like to return to?

- ❖ The first day - to experience the excitement and anticipation of entering a completely new phase of my life again.

- ❖ The first day. My first day really inspired me to learn about the intricate world we all live in. The University of Cape Town is a highly political university, in which many social issues are addressed almost on a daily basis. I realised this on my first day, and I felt as if I left my "school bubble" and finally understood the social/political issues that South Africa faces. This resulted in me becoming a lot more open minded and more "woke"'.

- ❖ My first one. Part of me would love to try it from the beginning again, but there's no point in looking backwards when the only way to go is forward.

- ❖ The First Day - to relive the sense of awe and trepidation.

- ❖ The very first day of orientation where I realised that the stream I picked was not exactly what I thought it was.

- ❖ The freshers week in 2019.

- ❖ First week of First Year, to get involved in more extra-curricular activities.

- ❖ First few weeks, when I was first getting to know my friends.

- ❖ I would like to return to the very first day of my arrival at my dorm/residence. I had a feeling that I was right where I needed to be, and that I would be just fine. There was nerves, but I was also excited.

- ❖ First Year - Springboks won the World Cup and aced an economics exam just after.

- First Year, when the workload was light and fun.

- The last day of my first year. We went to the beach to welcome the summer and had a hell of a time.

- First portfolio submission.

- I would return to the day before the first utterance of the word Covid-19, sometime late in 2019 or early in 2020, in the days when we took normalcy for granted and didn't know how lucky we were.

- The week before lockdown 2020.

- The first day back when we didn't have to wear masks after 2 years. Seeing people's smiles!

- I'd return to the day the first lockdown got announced. I was doing a module, and we were told to go home early because Leo Varadkar announced a nationwide lockdown effective immediately. I was happy to get an extended midterm at the time, little did I know how extended that mid term would really be :(. If I knew what was in store for the world, I would've had more appreciation for the last day on campus for a year and a half.

- The first few weeks before lockdown.

- The start of Erasmus.

- The night of 20th June 2018, into the morning of the 21st June. After a 3ish week road trip along the Croatian coast and the Balkans, a group of 30ish people, including me, who lived in the same apartment block all arrived back to our dorm called "Druzba" (directly translates to Comrade which was a bit ominous but strangely appropriate.) in Bratislava, Slovakia. Our floor was only for resident Erasmus students which made it incredibly special (and very loud from excessive partying!). We were one big loud, debauchery infused family. This particular night marked the end of our 10-month Erasmus adventure and the eve of my 21st birthday. We played music, drank cheap beer and reminisced of the amazing year we had. We were a community of European students who had become friends (and sometimes a bit more) for life, sharing the happiest year of our lives to date together! Everyone's doors were open, as we floated around the floor, laughing and hugging and deciding what countries we'll visit next for our reunions. :)

❖ Halloween night in my Erasmus year in Madrid.

❖ Playing cards against humanity with my friends on a Saturday evening on discord during lockdown.

❖ I would like to return to either my first year or my third year when I went for my exchange.

❖ None. I'm happy to move onto the next part of my life.

❖ I prefer to live in the moment but if I had to go back, a particular Friday of my MSc in semester one. It was one of those days that the lecturer was interesting, the girls were all giddy and all my mates ended up going for pints and DMCs (as we often did) in the college bar.

❖ Any day when I took the time to go for a chicken roll in Centra and have a quiet lunch with my friends.

❖ My last day of lectures before exams started- it was very sunny and everyone was in a good mood. :)

❖ Watching the football in the sun in our front garden.

❖ The day my friends and I sat on the grass by the lake under the hot sun relaxing and forgetting about all our lectures and assignments for a bit.

❖ Trinity Ball 2019.

❖ The day I first met my now best friend.

❖ The last few weeks of school before graduation - each day was idyllic.

❖ When my sister who lives abroad came to visit for the first time. I was 2 weeks away from finishing my course. The campus was buzzing with life (as it does when the sun sporadically shines in Ireland) as we sat by the "secret" lake & we went to watch a concert in the Olympia Theatre that evening.

❖ None, I enjoyed it to the max and would like to keep it as memories.

❖ There were a series of days in 2021 when our university caught on fire and it was a tragedy. I got stuck in with helping raise funding for those affected and I absolutely loved being able to help those affected. It was a difficult time, but I learnt how much I loved helping and serving others and I'd go back to that day to experience the joy of serving others like that again.

Recall your most vivid college memory.

❖ Standing at the top of a ski slope in Switzerland, on my first time going down a slope solo. I got two buzzes on my phone, one from my now girlfriend and one an update on my dream masters. The nerves and anticipation from the email, combined with the butterflies from the text is something, on top of fear from being on top of a slope was a feeling I will never forget.

❖ If I had to choose a memory in university, it'd probably be week 0 of First Year going to orientation events. It is a vivid memory in that I didn't really know what was going on, but I was okay with that, but it also taught me a lot about which friendships are more valuable.

❖ Exhibiting my most personal selection of photographic work [about having Autism] to date with my fellow classmates in a public gallery space.

❖ Honestly, when the whole class went from Bilbao to Madrid for a week and we partied so hard.

❖ Walking to class from the parking above campus, on an especially cold morning, listening to Juice Wrld and feeling especially sorry for myself; realising that I was not passionate about what I thought I was passionate about, that I hated what I was studying, that I was generally doing the wrong thing with my life, that I was depressed, and that I would have to figure out what it was that I should do.

❖ First day - everyone goes to the Clubhouse. As if it's the most normal thing in the world that there's a pub on campus. Unbelievable for an Erasmus student!

❖ Winning a cup final for UCD Men's Hockey, with all my friends, then celebrating as a team later on.

❖ Evening drinks on my terrace whilst on Erasmus are probably the most vivid memory.

Recall your most vivid college memory.

- ❖ Losing my virginity.

- ❖ Meeting for my first ever blind date on campus. It went unexpectedly well, we now live together and are moving to America in 3 months.

- ❖ Our BIS ball in 2019, we all got dressed up in fancy ball gowns and went for dinner and danced the night away!

- ❖ Surprising my college friends in Barcelona while on placement abroad (they had figured out I was coming anyway).

- ❖ Doing a roll over and going into college, putting a naggin into coffee cups and spending the whole day in college locked with all my friends - I think it was freshers week.

- ❖ Waking up for a 9 am lecture after yet another shift working till 3 am. First-year was no sleep but it paid for pints. (:

- ❖ Hiding from the guards while trying to shoot on the streets during quarantine.

- ❖ My most vivid College memory is when my university beat our biggest rivals Duke University in the national semi-final for college basketball last year. I've never seen our student body so united. We felt together for the first time in a long time due to Covid.

- ❖ Going travelling alone for 2 months, developed my independence a lot.

- ❖ Making a movie for a compsci module where a serial killer murders financially irresponsible students.

- ❖ A trip to Amsterdam with friends. We stayed in a loft with a balcony and took a trip to the grocery store to buy an assortment of cheap foodstuffs. We spent the night playing games, drinking wine and savouring our last few hours in Amsterdam before having to catch a 5am flight back to Dublin.

- ❖ A lecturer telling us we had to learn assembly language even though it would be of little to no use in our professional career.

❖ While quite hard to narrow it down to just one, a core memory that stands out for me was participating in the James Joyce Maidens Debating Competition. I was an avid debater in primary school and did Model United Nations for 2 years in secondary school, but as time went on, I slowly lost my confidence. Pushing myself outside my comfort zone and partaking in this university level debating competition helped restore faith in myself and my abilities.

❖ Getting word that I was approved to go on exchange to The University of Melbourne.

❖ Meeting my group of friends for the first time at the bar, I felt like I was in the right place immediately.

❖ The crowd of people chatting in the hallway, followed by the silence of the corridors after everyone got to their lecture.

❖ During the summer when Covid first hit, I was balancing my career in sport, an internship and college assignments which pushed me to work hard from 6 in the morning till 10 at night every weekday from June till mid-August.

❖ My first and last days.

I remember being absolutely terrified on day 1, not knowing anyone at all and having moved to a completely different province. It was a daunting but exciting first day with doors fully open for new experiences.

The last day was filled with nostalgia. Having achieved something I had worked toward for the last 4 years and then not knowing what to expect next. It was a beautiful thing to experience it with those very people I did not know on day 1, but by the end of it, we were all brothers and will remain so forever.

❖ Leaving campus for the final time before the Covid-19 pandemic took hold.

❖ Being reunited with First Year friends for our general maths lectures. I don't get to see them anymore so it was nice to share a class with them post Covid.

❖ A kick I made with such intent behind the action; it was to win my final bout during the Dublin Intercollegiate Karate Tournament.

❖ My best friends and I spent the New Year together after one in our group passed away due to cancer. Although he died too soon & it was an extremely tough period, we celebrated his life & all of the lives he touched. After the funeral with his family, we rented an Airbnb together & told stories as we reminisced but also realised that he'll always live on in our hearts.

❖ Setting off the fire alarm because I was drying my hair too high and the steam apparently triggered the alarm.

❖ Collaborative study sessions with my friends where we laughed and taught one another economics' concepts (often minutes before a test).

❖ Any ball I've ever been to. They've all sort of merged into one.

❖ Any day we played block cricket for hours in the sun! Chatting absolute nonsense with the lads.

❖ The first night out I had with my best friend who I met in college, it is a memory we both share and will never forget.

❖ Winning the minor cup.

❖ Going on our course trip to Barcelona 9-13th March 2020. Covid was just becoming a reality, we left Ireland with not a care in the world. We came home and had to self-isolate for 2 weeks and we never left the whole country went into lockdown.

❖ Having my movie shown to the entire course.

❖ Renting an apartment beside college for 3 months and moving out with two college friends at the end of the 2021 college year. More memories were made in those three months than in a full year of Covid. Strobe lights, cocktail parties, wine nights, adventures, love, friends. Woodbine House is my most vivid college memory.

❖ Coming back every September and catching up with everyone. Everyone would use their summer differently. It always fascinated me what everyone got up to.

❖ Getting called out by the lecturer for sleeping in the front row of a calculus lecture.

❖ The feeling of passing one of my stats courses - never thought I could do it but the relief and happiness I felt after that course was finished stands out so clearly.

❖ Playing board games in the International Students Orientation Week in First Year - where I met some of my best college friends.

❖ My first time in the film studio.

❖ There are so many!! My most recent one would be sitting at the steps of Botany Bay at 3am drinking whiskey.

❖ Playing soccer for the university under the stadium lights.

❖ Being in First Year in the study centre and looking out into a rainy Oxford Road, I don't know why but it does also sum up my time there quite well.

❖ I struggle to answer this question. It's such a blur with so many memories. I wish my past self wrote some of them down.

❖ My English lectures remain particularly vivid in my memory. The lecturers were always incredibly inspiring and managed to engage the class which made for such lively and thought-provoking debate.

❖ The day of my final submission for my undergraduate degree. In true college fashion I left this assignment till the very last minute. With just 15 minutes left, I did one final proofread of my assignment and clicked the submit button. I cleared my tabs, shut down my computer and went out for a walk. A very anticlimactic ending to a gruelling 4 years.

Recall your most vivid college memory.

- ❖ Lads—I've been in college for 10 years—there are too many…

- ❖ I was in my senior freshman year and was the sports officer in the Junior Common Room of my student residence. My birthday party fell during refreshers week, and had been a rager the night before - with loads of UV paint. I had never felt closer to so many people in this world. I also had met the love of my life, and girlfriend to this day, that week. I was walking over to see her the following morning when one of my lecturers, an assistant warden, offered to drive me to college for my new module. Covered in paint, wearing ragged clothes, and wreaking of jagerbombs, I humbly complied. God knows what we talked about in the car. I arrived outside the seminar room and couldn't bring myself to go in. Hopping back into a taxi in rush hour traffic Dublin the hangover starts to set in. Return to my apartment and find the place destroyed with UV paint. Starting the lengthy process of cleaning it up and I get a call - "Your grandmother has cancer, and only has a few months left to live."

What one principle would you have told yourself to live by before beginning university?

- ❖ Make the most of every opportunity and don't be afraid to get involved. I do feel I immersed myself in the university experience to a reasonable extent, but there were many chances I did not jump at which I feel could have enriched my life even more. For example, be it not participating in a competition because I had notions of not being good enough, or avoiding certain social events because I was worried I would be isolated the whole night. But your time in university is short-lived, and had I known the majority of it would have been taken by COVID, the primary principle I wish I had told myself would be to not be afraid and get involved, because there's never anything to lose, but only to gain by getting out there more.

- ❖ Gratitude. It's easy to focus on what we don't have, but being grateful for what we do brings a level of optimism. Optimism isn't about solely neglecting the bad. But accepting it, and finding the positive solution out of the situation.

- ❖ To be more courageous in my pursuit of self-discovery / embracing new experiences (culturally and academically) as being more open to getting to know new and diverse individuals.

- ❖ Go in open-minded and say yes to everything you can.

- ❖ Don't chase money, chase inner happiness. - I personally thought my degree would make me rich. Today I want to be rich in life's experiences.

- ❖ People are key to your experience in university. Learning to understand what drives people to do what they do will help immensely with both your school experience and social experience at university.

- ❖ Most important is that I am happy monetary compensation should not be the first priority.

What one principle would you have told yourself to live by before beginning university?

❖ Spend time with people you feel valued and understood by, choose your friends more wisely.

❖ There's no point in being shy, be weird!! You'll make more friends that way.

❖ You are the only one who can change, and improve yourself, and this will be a process that takes time and work, but it's going to be worth it.

❖ Seek discomfort - that's when you reach a level of growth. First Year was more about being as comfortable as possible, now I strive to become comfortable with the uncomfortable.

❖ Work on your own personal projects as well as academic ones.

❖ Be careful with your heart and don't put up with people who aren't careful with yours.

❖ Once you begin sweating, don't stop there. Keep sweating until you're drenched & only then do you know that your work is done.

❖ Your work doesn't need to be 100% perfect all the time. It's fine to have loose edges, if anything it gives you and your work more character.

❖ Don't take yourself so seriously, and don't be so hard on yourself.

❖ Maximise novelty.

❖ Enjoy being a college student but also work hard. It's quite easy to get good grades if you put your head down, and it's worth it in the end.

❖ There won't be any vacation in the next years.

❖ The joy of university is the flexibility it allows you, so take advantage of it. Take a day off if you need to, don't over-work yourself, and don't let yourself get overwhelmed by it all, because it is all manageable.

What one principle would you have told yourself to live by before beginning university?

❖ There is no difference between a 4.20 GPA & a 3.68 GPA at the end of the day.

❖ Work hard now, so you don't regret not working hard enough later.

❖ Past papers are better than good notes.

❖ Do not compare yourself to others in terms of their abilities to succeed. We're all at different levels when it comes to assimilating information. We all have different paths to walk, the one that has to walk it is ultimately you. The most critical thing to understand and value in this process is that you are constantly learning, if you have done better than yesterday you are already winning.

❖ You become like the five people you spend the most time with.

❖ It's never too early and never too late.

❖ Development is observing yours and others mistakes, thus learning from them. Leads to sincere growth.

❖ Focus on improving yourself in all aspects of life, not just in your academic one. College is a place to make life-long memories and there are so many opportunities to do that.

❖ Say yes to everything and any opportunity that comes your way, even if it seems like it's something you never would have done before- it will lead to new friends and even better opportunities than you could have ever imagined for yourself.

❖ You alone decide what has value to you.

❖ Discipline. I struggled to find a consistent routine in my first two years at university - I was not disciplined in getting my work done in the time that I needed it done, and as such it lead me to stress unnecessarily.

❖ You're not nearly as ugly and stupid as you think.

What one principle would you have told yourself to live by before beginning university?

- ❖ If I was to start my journey again, I would tell myself to keep my head down on my own work, and realise nobody else can do the work for you.

- ❖ It's not about your answer, it's about how the examiner interprets and values your writing.

- ❖ Do what you like, not what you think you like.

- ❖ Throw yourself into it, because you'll get out what you put in.

- ❖ It's okay to be different or have a different path, don't let fomo get to you.

- ❖ Trying things you don't like will help you find what you do.

- ❖ Get your work done before enjoying yourself.

- ❖ Move out of your comfort zone.

- ❖ Try to have as much fun as you possibly can.

- ❖ It's okay to be a sore thumb - I've learned that standing out & being my own person brings so much more opportunity than trying to morph into a group.

- ❖ To try as many things as possible and interact with different people as much as I can.

- ❖ Keep going, don't give up, pursue your true self.

- ❖ It's okay to take time to chill. If anything, it's important.

- ❖ Don't chase people who want out of your life, spend the time bettering yourself.

- ❖ Live in the present.

- ❖ Expand your circle.

❖ I would have told myself to never be afraid to seek help from my peers and professors.

❖ Make a good work/life balance and stick to it.

❖ Make the most of every day. You never know when your uni career will come to an end or get interrupted by something unexpected.

❖ Be kind to everyone, everyone is going through something and come from different walks of life.

❖ Positivity fuels productivity.

❖ Be driven by your curiosity and not passion or perfectionism.

❖ Not letting others define who I am.

❖ Say yes as much as possible.

❖ Be careful with your words, and speak purposefully, with intention.

❖ Organise your time and plan effectively.

❖ If you can't balance work and social life, forget about your social life for a while and completely focus on work just until you get back up on your feet. You won't have any regrets in the long run.

❖ You are the only person responsible for your happiness & prosperity.

❖ Catch up regularly before any assignments or exams due. A first-class honour only needs 3.68 and any scores exceeded are wasted.

❖ Join more societies.

❖ Think about what is meaningful to you regarding your education rather than what is expedient, empty, and meaningless. In pursuit of expedient and immediate goals, it is easy to overlook the importance of cultivating friendships and acquiring knowledge about topics that evoke our interest, even if they are not directly relevant to our course of study.

❖ Have fun and do what you feel like doing at that moment in time.

❖ Make the most of the flexibility and opportunity university gives you!

❖ Being yourself in comfortable situations is not enough, do it ALWAYS.

❖ Don't be afraid to try new things and immerse yourself into unknown things.

❖ Express gratitude regularly. You might get hit by a bus tomorrow.

❖ "To let myself go during bouts of discomfort. Recently (since finishing college) when feeling a bit overwhelmed and lost, I walk/run and do a quick metaphysical inventory;

Consciousness that this is a planet and of the sky and clouds.

Consciousness that I am lucky to be here.

Consciousness that I got myself here.

Consciousness that I am thankful."

It helps me to feel grounded and this kind of meditation would have been helpful I'm sure in college.

❖ Start assignments about a week or two earlier than you would normally.

❖ Don't do drugs :)

❖ Relax and have the craic.

❖ Take it as it goes and learn what you can.

❖ That the piece of paper you will spend 4 years chasing will never define you, and there are other opportunities outside of the university degree bubble.

❖ Choose the college not the course.

❖ Serve others without the expectation of being served in return.

What one principle would you have told yourself to live by before beginning university?

❖ Your propensity to succeed is negatively correlated with how much you celebrate.

❖ Whatever seems hard isn't too bad once you're in it.

❖ The only certainty is uncertainty. Embrace it with a sense of curiosity but with the knowledge that I won't ever have all the answers.

❖ To be true to who I am and not be someone else.

❖ Almost nothing of what you worry about will actually happen.

❖ Stay true to yourself.

❖ Look to impact your circle.

❖ Don't be afraid to put yourself out there, even if you fail or get rejected, never give up. Failure and rejection don't feel great in the moment, but in hindsight, it builds character, perseverance and resilience.

❖ Be yourself and ask questions.

❖ Always give 100%, never settle for the bare minimum because one day you'll need to give 100% and you won't know how.

❖ Do not get caught up in what others are doing - you can only do so much yourself.

❖ Be honest with yourself about whether you enjoy what you are studying and don't be afraid to change your degree. Focus on trying to use the time at Uni to find out what you enjoy doing, rather than worrying about whether you are doing "the right thing" - there is no "right thing".

❖ Take every opportunity you get, don't limit yourself. Dream big.

❖ Ask more questions.

❖ Grades aren't as important as everyone says, as soon as you have that first job nobody then looks at your university grades. The most important things you should do is try new things, grow, develop and make as many connections as you can.

❖ One conversation can change your life, speak to more people.

❖ Articulate less, execute more.

❖ Think deeply using your brain rather than your emotions about decisions which may change your life.

❖ Learned that if you are not entirely sure do not take the risk.

❖ Most of the time, go with your gut.

❖ Growth happens at the edges.

❖ To trust my instincts if I felt capable of doing the task.

❖ You cannot always rely on others.

❖ To not always trust other's opinions, and to be responsible for myself.

❖ To live by anything but fear. We all feel fear, that is why I dislike the term 'fearless', but I have learned pushing through it over and over and over is the best way to live.

Remember

The Past encourages us to **Remember**.

As much as we can believe something theoretically, our experiences are what allow us to learn about ourselves. The reflections clearly show pain, joy, failure, success, discomfort and passion. The Past often tells us what doesn't work before we conclude what does. The questions sent us down memory lane, helping us recall negative experiences, lessons learned, and nostalgic memories. It's worth mentioning that while we have identified recurring themes in the answers, there is a diversity of thought. As a reader, trying to absorb what life is like for students based on hundreds of perspectives can be overwhelming. Take these reflections and words of advice with a pinch of salt. Apply those relevant to you. Most importantly, we'd recommend you answer the same questions to see how far you've come on your journey.

Remember where you were.

Meaningful Highlight 2
You can understand someone's intellect by the books they had on their bookshelf

12 Rules for Life - Jordan Peterson

A General Theory of Oblivion - Jose Eduardo Agualusa

A Man Called Ove - Fredrik Backman

A Sound of Thunder - Ray Bradbury

Adaptive Markets - Andrew W. Lo

All the Devils Are Here – Bethany McLean & Joe Nocera

Americanah - Chimamanda Ngozi Adichie

At the Bottom of Everything - Ben Dolnick

Atkins' Physical Chemistry - Keeler, De Paula & Atkins

Atomic Habits - James Clear

Beartown - Fredrik Backman

Beginner's Pluck - Liz Bohannon

Betting On a Darkie - Mteto Nyati

Being Mortal - Atul Gawande

Call Me By My True Names - Thich Nhat Hanh

Clean Code - Robert C. Martin

Contemporary Strategy Analysis - Robert M. Grant

Dark Matter - Blake Crouch

Deep Work - Cal Newport

Design For the Real World - Victor Papanek

Di-Volution - Herman Singh

Dune - Frank Herbert

Ecology of a Cracker Childhood - Janisse Ray

Econometric Analysis of Cross Section and Panel Data - Jeffrey Wooldridge

Everything I Know About Love: A Memoir - Dolly Alderton

You can understand someone's intellect by the books they had on their bookshelf

Factfullness - Hans Rosling

Feminist Theory: From Margin to Centre - Bell Hooks

Frankenstein - Mary Shelley

Give & Take - Adam Grant

Good Vibes, Good Life - Vex King

How to Stop Worrying and Start Living - Dale Carnegie

Humble Pi - Matt Parker

I Am Pilgrim - Terry Hayes

I Am Zlatan - Zlatan Ibrahimovic

I Write What I Like - Steve Biko

Influence: The Psychology of Persuasion - Robert B. Cialdini

Inner Engineering - Sadhguru

Insomniac City - Bill Hayes

Inspired - Marty Cagan

Introduction to Quantum Mechanics - David J. Griffiths

It's all in your head- Russ

Justice - Michael J. Sandel

Kafka on the Shore - Haruki Murakami

Klara and the Sun - Kazuo Ishiguro

Long Walk to Freedom - Nelson Mandela

Make Your Bed - William H. McRaven

Managing Your Own Learning at University - Aidan Moran

Man's Search for Meaning - Viktor Frankl

Mastery - Robert Greene

Meditations - Marcus Aurelius

Mindset - Dr. Carol S Dweck

Misbehaving - Richard Thaler

Neuroeconomics - Paul Glimcher

Neuromarketing - Morin & Renvoise

No Rules Rules - Meyer & Hastings

Noughts & Crosses - Malorie Blackman

Nudge: Improving Decisions about Health, Wealth, and Happiness - Thaler & Sunstein

Reflections

You can understand someone's intellect by the books they had on their bookshelf

On the Road - Jack Kerouac

Outliers - Malcolm Gladwell

Papillon - Henri Charriére

Pass Your Driving Test - Kathleen Comerford

Permanent Record - Edward Snowden

Power of Geography - Tim Marshall

Resilience: Hard-Won Wisdom for Living a Better Life - Eric Greitens

Rich Dad Poor Dad - Kiyosaki & Lechter

Sell Like Crazy - Sabri Suby

Shantaram - Gregory David Roberts

Shoe Dog - Phil Knight

Silence - Shūsaku Endo

Steppenwolf - Hermann Hesse

Surrounded By Idiots - Thomas Erikson

The 7 Spiritual Laws of Success - Deepak Chopra

The 10x Rule - Grant Cardone

The Alchemist - Paolo Coelho

The Art of War - Sun Tzu

The Bell Jar - Sylvia Plath

The Boy, The Mole, The Fox and The Horse - Charlie Mackesy

The Country of White Lilies - Grigory Spiridonovich Petrov

The Celestine Prophecy - James Redfield

The Daily Stoic - Ryan Holiday

The Defining Decade - Meg Jay

The Fish That Ate the Whale: The Life and Times of America's Banana King - Rich Cohen

The God Delusion - Richard Dawkins

The Great Gatsby - F. Scott Fitzgerald

The Hand of Darkness - Ursula K. LeGuin

The Hero's Journey - Joseph Campbell

The Law Nutshell Series - Various Authors

The Lessons of History - Ariel Durant & Will Durant

You can understand someone's intellect by the books they had on their bookshelf

The New Business Road Test - John Mullins

The Nolan Variations - Tom Shone

The Panopticon - Jenni Fagan

The Perks of Being a Wallflower - Stephen Chbosky

The Power of Geography - Tim Marshall

The Quran

The Reluctant Fundamentalist - Mohsin Hamid

The Richest Man in Babylon - George S. Clason

The Righteous Mind - Jonathan Haidt

The Road Less Travelled - Scott Peck

The Secret Life of Bees - Sue Monk Kidd

The Shining - Stephen King

The Stranger - Albert Camus

The Subtle Art of Not Giving a F*ck - Mark Manson

The Worldly Philosophers - Robert Heilbroner

The Young Entrepreneur's Playbook - Lindile Xoko

Thermodynamics: An Engineering Approach - Boles & Çengel

This Side of Paradise - F. Scott Fitzgerald

To Kill a Mockingbird - Harper Lee

Tuesdays With Morrie - Mitch Albom

Volkswagen Blues - Jacques Poulin

Ways of Seeing - John Berger

What Is History? - EH Carr

Where the Crawdads Sing - Delia Owens

Whittled Away - Pádraic Fog

THE PRESENT

The Present encourages us to **Take Action.**

Take Action from where you are. This chapter provides insights into meaningful pastimes, changes in desire, best and worst aspects of university, comfort zone escapism, current priorities, and purchases that have provided disproportionate value relative to their cost.

The following is the Student View of **The Present**.

What pastime or hobby has a meaningful, tangible impact on your life?

❖ Writing. I have always loved to write, albeit it is something that I have left behind over the past few years yet is something that I need to revisit soon. I received Insomniac City, as a gift from my parents for my birthday a few years ago. A few days after receiving this gift, I flew to Italy to spend my summer teaching English. So, it was in Milan that I started to read this book and it would be only a short two weeks later that I would finish it in Verona, or little did I know that it would be another four months later re-reading it in my minute totalitarian-esque flat in Bratislava whilst cooking pasta for days on a hot plate (in my wardrobe, yes, such extravagant health and safety concerns). This book is my solace. I feel happiness. I feel tranquillity. I feel sadness. I feel depth. I am reminded of the importance of writing; the greatness of writing about what it is like to live today. I am reminded of the importance of adventure. The beauty and scale of this fascinating and perplexing life that we, as human beings are able to live. I am reminded of gratitude. I am reminded that we are all worthy, significant.

❖ I row for my university as a hobby. I love filling my time outside university hours with physical exercise as the endorphins and adrenaline make me more productive as well as feeling happy, if I'm feeling stressed from uni work.

❖ Sports, photography and videography, travelling.

❖ Video Games - Best stress relief.

❖ Lifting / Interpretive Dancing.

❖ Creating art/designs.

❖ Field hockey.

❖ People watching. The first thing I like to do when I arrive at a new travel destination is go to a big park & just observe life in this new place. It's always different in each place in so many aspects.

❖ Dancing.

❖ Cooking and baking.

❖ Journalling is a very impactful hobby that has become an essential part of my daily routine.

❖ Reading/Coding.

❖ Meditation - the way I think & act has much more clarification & direction.

❖ Walking always lifts my mood.

❖ Working out. Sometimes it really helps me to get rid of the bad feelings.

❖ I practise Karate, which has taught me values that I try to implement in my day to day.

❖ Playing the guitar.

❖ Making a regular commitment to go to the gym or exercise everyday.

❖ Yoga.

❖ Skiing.

❖ Coaching.

❖ Journaling!!!! I try to journal most days. It has helped me to deal with situations and problems easily and more maturely- it also helps me to be more patient and understanding of other people, which in turn improves my relationships with them. I can also understand myself and who I am a lot better, and be aware of the negative aspects of my personality that I need to work on.

What pastime or hobby has a meaningful, tangible impact on your life?

❖ Football.

❖ Hiking.

❖ Hockey.

❖ Cinematography.

❖ Gaelic Football.

❖ Keeping up to date with political and economic situations in every corner of the world helps me understand where people come from better.

❖ Judo and Martial arts in general.

❖ All things traditional Irish music! Playing in sessions, teaching, composing, and antiquarian book collecting.

❖ Volunteering Overseas. Volunteering really opened my mind to new cultures while being able to give back in a sustainable and ethical way.

❖ Kayaking in the open sea with friends.

❖ Basketball.

❖ Water Polo. I have played water polo since a young age and the sport is still in my life to this day. After leaving school, I put a lot of focus in coaching water polo and have slowly climbed the coaching ranks in South African schools water polo. This has led me to building significant relationships amongst the top water polo coaches in South Africa and the sport has kept me motivated throughout my years at university.

❖ Exercise- whenever life is sh*t exercise is a great way to take your mind off things.

❖ Writing poetry.

❖ Doing puzzles!

What pastime or hobby has a meaningful, tangible impact on your life?

- ❖ Surfing.

- ❖ Sports, playing and watching.

- ❖ Playing golf - it may not seem so meaningful, but there's nothing that can make me laugh like playing golf with my best friends and that sought of belly-laughing means so much to me.

- ❖ Reading books.

- ❖ Making music!

- ❖ Painting.

- ❖ Mountain Biking.

- ❖ Walking or listening to music.

- ❖ Adventuring.

- ❖ Sailing - It taught me grit and determination, that the route followed by most is not always the best and to back yourself when you believe you are correct even if that's contrary to crowds belief!

- ❖ Enactus.

- ❖ Visiting art galleries.

- ❖ Rugby.

- ❖ Powerlifting.

- ❖ Running.

- ❖ Photography, it lets me look at the world in a different light.

- ❖ Waking up in the morning & going for a run in nature, with no music, followed by a cold shower & a meditation. It has become my post-COVID routine - It aligns my intentions for the day, makes me feel great & allows me to be in touch with myself & what I want to achieve.

What are the best & worst aspects of life at university?

✓ The independence, making new friends, meeting people from all around the world.

✗ Letting a bad grade define your worth, university is so big that you can become too comfortable staying in your own bubble, trying to find that balance between college work, doing things that you love and social life.

✓ Social, meeting with new people who have similar views.

✗ The bureaucracy of university.

✓ Exposure to people from all walks of life. You are very much shaped by those that surround you.

✗ It's easy to develop an inferiority complex in college, especially in a competitive environment [this can be a double-edged sword, it either motivates you to do better or it magnifies your insecurities].

✓ You have loads of free time to learn different things only if you take advantage of it.

✗ Everyone learns the same thing.

✓ Always the people.

✗ Probably realising that all your education is directed towards making an economically productive individual out of yourself.

✓ Socialising and networking.

✗ I wish I had more opportunities to pick modules outside of my main study.

✓ Making friends for life.

✗ Paying a FORTUNE for accommodation each year as well as fees.

✓ The people you meet.

✗ The stress your lecturers put you under. It's not their fault but the curriculum needs some adjustments.

✓ Meeting new and different people all the time.

✗ The struggle to balance all aspects of my life and never feeling like I have enough time in the day.

✓ Making friends.

✗ Losing friends.

✓ The period is an amount of time carved out by society for you to learn freely in areas you wish to explore. You grow as a person at a rapid pace.

✗ Lack of practical implementation of theory/real-life experience when engaging with college material.

✓ Academics.

✗ Social life.

✓ You can do anything you want.

✗ You can do anything you want. Knowing what you want is difficult to find.

✓ Freedom, social life.

✗ Pressure.

✓ Making friends, social aspect, learning from highly skilled professors.

✗ The feeling of learning something primarily for an exam, rather than for enjoyment.

✓ Social life, interesting lectures, being around different people.

✗ Exams/assignments, travelling to university.

✓ I had a good bunch and nice people.

✗ Having f*ck all money.

✓ A lot of group work, you get to meet a lot of people.

✗ Can be overwhelming with assignments.

✓ Mixing with other people.

✗ Over excessive on drinking alcohol.

✓ Making new friends.

✗ Large lecture halls.

✓ Growing up.

✗ Growing up.

✓ Meeting incredible people and making friends for life. Having opportunities that I never saw possible. Growing as a lifelong learner (expanding on my knowledge).

✗ The lack of communication between the department and students. Pressure to know everything (no room for errors).

✓ The social aspect.

✗ The education approach.

✓ There is nobody to hold you accountable.

✗ There is nobody to hold you accountable.

✓ Societies: Amount of diverse people you meet and network you build. It's a time during which you know yourself better.

✗ Facing outdated education methods. The student body is quite polarised on issues.

✓ The friends you make, it's refreshing to make new friends apart from your childhood friends.

✗ Some of the methods of evaluation.

✓ You can choose.

✗ You can choose.

❖ There is always so much to do! Nights out with friends, competitions to take part in, training with sports club, society meetings, dates, essays, exams, deadlines. It's very easy to become overwhelmed and lost in all the things that college has to offer. The key is to understand that life is about trade-offs and that you can't do everything you want to. You can go out with your friends every night, but don't expect to be able to make it to every 9 AM lecture or get all your college work done. Or you can go to every lecture, do every reading and finish every essay a week in advance, but miss out on the fun of college life. It's all about getting the right balance that works best for you.

How do you break out of your comfort zone?

❖ I break out of my comfort zone by setting myself short term personal goals. For example, during orientation week, I set myself a goal to speak to 100 new people in 5 days. I went to various society events, nights out and even just spoke to people on the bus back from college. Initially it was excruciatingly uncomfortable, but the more I did it, the easier it became and I ended up making friends with people I still keep in touch with today!

❖ Understand what makes you uncomfortable, question it and then pursue what makes you uncomfortable.

❖ As an introvert, the best way for me is to push myself to go to more social events where I meet new people or to try out a new hobby.

❖ By being around people I know will inspire me to do more than I would on my own.

❖ I don't let such a zone to be established in the first place. This question is like saying love your enemy. Why would you label him your enemy in the first place and then go through the trouble of loving him?

❖ Forcing myself to talk to people.

❖ By having the fear in the back of my mind that if I don't break out of my comfort zone that I will stay the same and not improve in certain aspects of my life.

❖ Recognize the insignificant impacts of failure/rejection - contextualising the tangible positives and tangible negatives of the possible outcomes.

E.G. getting rejected from a job interview - you either get a job, or you fail but get one step closer to improving your odds/experience at getting another job.

❖ Try to speak to strangers and start the conversation.

❖ Travelling and talking to people with different mindset and background.

❖ I put myself in situations that make me uncomfortable.

❖ Launching myself into jobs in foreign countries because of Instagram ads.

❖ By expanding my skill sets and throw myself into something I've never tried before.

❖ Speaking up in lectures. it's not something that I like doing, but I'm always glad I did it afterwards.

❖ Music.

❖ By taking the path of most resistance. If I'm hungry, stay hungry for a while. If I want to stop exercising, go for 5 minutes more. If I don't want to speak up, speak up. I find I enjoy life so much more once I overcome these small hurdles.

❖ Talk to everyone, don't judge people.

❖ Introduce myself to someone new.

❖ If I'm home a lot I'll organise a night out to get out of the rut of being a homebody.

❖ Hitting the pain barrier in the form of intense exercise.

❖ Expand your skill set and throw yourself into something you've never tried before.

❖ Travelling.

❖ Embrace experiences with a high probability of failure that will result in personal growth, whatever the outcome.

❖ Solo travel - I have learned so much about myself, developed my own distinct identity & learned a whole lot about other cultures & perspectives. This hasn't come without a couple tricky situations, but it is so worth it. Once you do something once, the next time it's only easier.

❖ By saying yes to things you normally wouldn't try.

❖ By looking at things from a long-term perspective, if the end result seems satisfactory, then you just do what you have to do to get there.

❖ Initially, performing in front of people. It can still be uncomfortable, but it's a lot easier now than when I started.

❖ Setting a goal that is outside my comfort zone, once it's a goal I'm likely to work for it.

❖ Just doing things I don't want to do but that I need to/should. I don't have a method other than just forcing myself to do it with a smile lol.

❖ Start with an open mind and be optimistic about change.

❖ Social Climbing.

❖ By reminding myself that life is short and to step out of my comfort zone is to learn and grow as a human being.

❖ Meet new people and try new things.

❖ By attending an event of which I know no one there and talking with people I've never met.

❖ Anytime my heart rate increases & my inner voice tells me not to do something, I do it anyway for my benefit.

What purchase cost you less than €100 and added disproportionate value to your life?

❖ My cat Otis, got him for free off Done Deal and he's gas.

❖ May seem like a stupid answer, but a compact backpack I bought last year before I started cycling everyday. I have carried my laptop, gym clothes, earphones, stationery, food, etc. in that bag. All necessities I need for my daily life. Without it I wouldn't be able to enjoy myself. Earphones for music relevant to the activity I am doing. EDM for cycling, hardstyle music for the gym. Gym clothes to work out and stay fit, and to escape from the hardships of life for over an hour. Food to nourish and fuel me. The backpack acts as the glue that holds not only my items together, but my life together.

❖ My Spotify subscription.

❖ Definitely psychedelics. Having experimented with them during university, I am forever grateful for the unique perspectives they allowed me to tap into with regards to concepts of the self, the universe, love and spirituality.

❖ I wish I could say my eBook reader, cost me only €50, but with college I haven't been able to do outside reading as much as I'd hoped. If there's one habit that I wish to develop in the next year, it would be to read more.

❖ My first guitar.

❖ A pair of Nike shoes. They were the first big purchase (over $50 USD) that I had ever done. I saved my money to do this and it showed me the value of money.

❖ My Birkenstocks.

❖ Laptop stand. So good for your neck posture.

What purchase cost you less than €100 and added disproportionate value to your life?

- ❖ Renting a computer in an internet Cafe in the 2011 days.

- ❖ My football boots.

- ❖ Slightly over €100, but a second-hand camera.

- ❖ Ryanair tickets.

- ❖ Wall-mounted bottle opener.

- ❖ My thermal insulated water bottle, I take that thing everywhere with me.

- ❖ My journal and a good pen.

- ❖ My second-hand bike added a lot of value to my life. Cost me around 80 euro but gave me so much independence from buses etc.

- ❖ A notebook – the single most useful thing I have ever bought.

- ❖ 2nd hand books.

- ❖ A favour that I asked of my classmate to write my test to pass the exam.

- ❖ A plane ticket.

- ❖ A type of pen from an Italian supermarket called UPIM - the pen no longer exists. :(

- ❖ Amazon Kindle.

- ❖ Going bungee jumping off the Bloukrans Bridge in South Africa.

- ❖ Gym membership.

- ❖ Tickets to a gig.

- ❖ A camera lens.

- ❖ A football.

What purchase cost you less than €100 and added disproportionate value to your life?

- ❖ My Driver's Licence. It's ridiculous that you have to pay any money for it, but it's definitely worth it…

- ❖ Clean code book.

- ❖ My boxing gloves.

- ❖ Vitamin D supplements.

- ❖ Air Fryer!

- ❖ A yearly diary.

- ❖ Books.

- ❖ My laptop monitor. It really increased my productivity during lockdown.

- ❖ My sensory stones - they help reduce stress & anxiety levels. Free from our beautiful world!

- ❖ My bike. It saves me so much money in the city and can even be faster than public transport.

- ❖ My jersey of my favourite team.

- ❖ Entrance to the nightclub where I ended up meeting my now boyfriend.

- ❖ Anti-Noise Foam Earplugs.

- ❖ Swimming socks and gloves for the winter (Bye Raynaud's Syndrome).

- ❖ Any flight to somewhere new.

- ❖ Blackout curtains.

List your top 3 priorities at present.

1) Academics (I am trying to downgrade this to second place) **2)** My own personal growth (cheesy and true) **3)** Family and friends (ALSO cheesy but true)

1) Roar incredibly loudly for the rest of my 20's **2)** Gain valuable work & travel experience **3)** Feeling discomfort at least once a day (talking to a stranger, speaking up in class, taking a cold shower, etc.)

1) Enjoying the present moment and it's happy moments **2)** Take care of my mental and physical health **3)** Love myself

1) Setting myself up for the future financially **2)** Family **3)** Enjoying my youth while I can

1) Get a mattress **2)** Get competent at work **3)** Learn everything I can

1) Be grateful **2)** Never stop learning **3)** Make a positive impact on the world

1) Training **2)** Work **3)** Future endeavours

1) Move outside of Dublin **2)** Start my investment portfolio **3)** Meet new people

1) Living a life in line with my values **2)** Finding stability **3)** Forming meaningful relationships

1) Midterm exams **2)** Final exams **3)** Post-university arrangements

1) Find a good internship for the summer. **2)** Achieve a First Class Honours in my undergrad **3)** Finish my undergrad and get the hell out of college

1) Personal Ambitions **2)** Investment Portfolio **3)** Habit formation

1) Maintaining my health **2)** Solidifying my independence **3)** Learning/education

List your top 3 priorities at present.

1) Find a new job in a new city **2)** Play a live show with new songs **3)** Take a leap of faith

1) My Mind **2)** My future career **3)** Finishing my last set of exams the way I want

1) Graduate and get into my dream university for my Master's degree **2)** Learn to love myself more **3)** Spend as much time as possible with my friends in Ireland before leaving the country

1) Getting started in my job **2)** Getting my degree finished **3)** Enjoying my summer

1) Finishing off my last semester in a strong way **2)** Starting my masters in September **3)** Taking life day by day

1) Live in the present **2)** Challenge yourself **3)** Do what you enjoy

1) Grades **2)** Relationships **3)** Pursuing my dream job

1) Family **2)** Myself **3)** College

1) Enjoy life as much as possible **2)** Learn to keep myself safe and in control **3)** Keep my family and friends happy

1) Family and Loved Ones **2)** Work **3)** Experiencing the world

1) Travel **2)** Sport **3)** What path I want to take with my career

1) Be happy **2)** Be financially stable **3)** Stop stressing

1) Family **2)** Career **3)** Travel

1) Staying in the present **2)** Creating new memories, experience and stories **3)** Not giving up on my current adventure

What do you desire? How have your desires changed since your first year of university?

- ❖ In First Year, I constantly desired things that I thought would make me 'happier' (a holiday, a girlfriend, more money), but I've come to realise now that happiness is just a state of mind. Now, I desire to become a better person who offers more to society, and I can do that while being happy.

- ❖ I desire to live a life of passion, purpose and impact. I've always desired this, even since First Year. What changed from First Year is "where" I thought I would live this life out in the sense that I saw myself achieving this in a corporate environment, but now I don't think the corporate environment is the space that I will be able to build that life in.

- ❖ Travelling never changes, having someone by my side, that changed, finally.

- ❖ At the start of college I was more focused on the short run - getting through the day/week, so those were my desires. Now that I am at the end of my time in college, my desires shift to more long-term future focused ideals.

- ❖ I want to live my life on my own terms. In my first year of study, I was living based on what other people expected and to other people's standards which is no way to live.

- ❖ Success in vague terms, essentially a strong career, but now I have a better idea of how to approach it.

- ❖ I desire to do what I love and not just because there is a guarantee.

- ❖ To be happy with how life turns out for me. It was sort of the same at the start of university but happiness has a different meaning to me now than what it did when I was 18.

❖ I suppose meaning, as opposed to money at the start of college.

❖ Stability. They have changed significantly since I began at 18.

❖ I have a strong desire for freedom. This has changed since I began college when I was more focussed on money. Money is still very important, but now I know why I seek wealth, and the reason for that is the freedom it brings.

❖ I desire to be content with who I am.

❖ My desires have not changed, I still seek to make money and retire early so I could enjoy life.

❖ Life's ambition and desire for me is to try my best to enjoy the transience of time as best as I can. My goals and priorities are constantly shifting, but my main outlook shift since my first year at university has been to enjoy the mundane normality of daily life instead of always looking at what is next.

❖ Strong friendships, which largely hasn't changed since. If anything, I value the health of my friends and family even more.

❖ To be successful, and make a difference in the world. I first thought success meant having lots of money, but now I want to be successful in a way that people look up to me and feel inspired.

❖ Now I'm more practical and focused on outcomes.

❖ Move away and experience living by yourself.

❖ Presently, I desire to start up my own charity. When I started college, the word "career" seemed distant. Far away enough to allow me to comfortably explore what I could want from a career, but close enough that I felt like I should try to begin figuring this kind of thing out. When I thought of 'desire' as a First Year uni student, I thought of sunny travels, rom-com type romance and long-lasting friendships. As a law student, desire was being the best in my class and hoping to someday work for a fancy firm that I really didn't know anything about but figured that it would be good because it was expected! I stuck close to my degree by way of completing internships in law firms, volunteering in my uni's free legal aid clinic and even working for Amnesty as a fundraiser for migrant rights. I thought I might like to end up working in EU policy in Brussels as did many of my peers, however volunteering in charities and NGOs ignited my appetite for a career in this sector. Gradually, I noticed my desires changing as they became more real and meaningful to me. My Erasmus year allowed me to travel and meet people from different cultures with different perspectives. I felt like I was growing in a way that felt exciting; new countries, new people, new food, new opportunities, new relationships, it was a journey that I never wanted to end. I felt clear headed and in control because of how happy I was from these experiences and again, my desires began to broaden. I knew that I needed to cultivate the professional skills that would enable me to truly make a difference. Intrinsically, I decided to extend my time in Ireland, rather than pursuing a masters abroad because of the passion I had for a charity that I worked in. So I decided to be practical by taking a position working in management consultancy whilst volunteering. During this time, I learned how important good leadership and governance is for the operational functions of an org, and to motivate people to assert the best version of themselves because sometimes motivation and a passion to the cause isn't always enough for people to excel. These experiences have shaped the path that I find myself on and after a few years in this charity and a stint in the corporate world, I am excited to see what comes next and to see how my desires will continue to shift over time.

❖ A comfortable life in terms of money and health.

❖ I desire to live life and not look back with regret. Each has their own interpretation of that saying.

❖ I desire to always challenge myself into creating great experiences. I also care less about getting rich than I used to, that is what my focus was at the start of uni. I want to be around the people I love as much as possible, and to go out and make new connections and experiences as much as possible too.

❖ I still desire to be successful, being able to take care of people I care about, help causes I believe in while being happy and fulfilled along the way. My desires haven't changed much, I think the only difference is now knowing how much harder it is to achieve than I believed during my first year.

❖ I desire the feeling of being present and being in the moment. Since my first year at university, I have slowly focused on practising mindfulness and looking inwards. I have done this by meditating, exercising and journaling. This has been a hard journey for me since I've struggled to get a proper routine, but this year I have finally learnt to practise mindfulness every morning and I feel the benefits of it throughout my day.

❖ I desire freedom. I used to think I wanted a good stable job, I now realise that is not the key to happiness. Do something you like, not something that makes you be respected.

❖ I'm very ambitious and determined. Since I started college, my goal was to become a lawyer and that hasn't changed.

❖ I desire success (on my own terms) and peace. When I first came to university, I wanted to be a top academic overachiever, much like I was in high school. I quickly learned that this new chapter in my life demanded the unlearning of that behaviour and the learning of new things, such as allowing myself to live, and have fun, and to be of service to others.

❖ In the short term, I desire to continue enjoying life through new and old human connections. I think I felt similarly in my first year of university but I was less open-minded and more judgmental then which presumably held me back from opportunities.

Take Action

We use the past as a foundation for who we have become, but the present is about action. We often treat others based on how we treat ourselves, so how we consciously spend our time becomes very important. We found it interesting to analyse what contributors desire. Many have changed their view on happiness over the past few years. But the biggest question we think arising from the chapter is: Are your priorities aligned with your desires, and are your priorities & desires both aligned to how you spend your time? It's one thing to say it, but another to do it. Often doing requires us to escape our comfort zones. And when we leave comfort behind, we grow. So, when you're feeling uncomfortable, use the discomfort as motivation to keep doing what you're doing. There's no better time than now to do it.

Take Action from where you are.

Meaningful Highlight 3
A good movie is remembered as vividly as some of your best memories.

12 Angry Men

14 Peaks

3 Idiots

A Beautiful Mind

About Time

All Dogs Go to Heaven

Almost Famous

Amelie

Apocalypse Now

Avatar

Babyteeth

Back To the Future

Beautiful Boy

Boyhood

Brother Bear

Captain Fantastic

Cars

Chasing Mavericks

Click

Coach Carter

Coco

Crash

Cry Freedom

Dazed and Confused

Dead Poets Society

Donnie Darko

Don't Look Up

Eat Pray Love

Ferris Bueller's Big Day Out

Fight Club

Finding Dory

Forrest Gump

Freaky Friday

Freedom Writers

Good Will Hunting

Green Book

Hair

Hot Fuzz

Howl's Moving Castle

I'm Not Scared

Inside Out

Interstellar

Invictus

It's a Wonderful Life

Jeen-Yuhs - Part 1 Through 3

Joker

La Grande Bellezza

La vita è bella

Last Night in SoHo

Les Intouchables

A good movie is remembered as vividly as some of your best memories.

Life Itself	The Blind Side
Life of Pi	The Boat That Rocked
Lion	The Boy Who Harnessed the Wind
Little Women	The Breakfast Club
Marriage Story	The Commitment
Martín (Hache)	The Grand Budapest Hotel
Meet the Robinsons	The Great Hack
Mommy	The Guard
Moonlight	The Lion King
My Octopus Teacher	The Lives of Others
My Sister's Keeper	The Lorax
Nomadland	The Lord of the Rings
Oliver and Company	The Matrix
Parasite	The Perks of Being a Wallflower
Patch Adams	The Pursuit of Happiness
Peanut Butter Falcon	The Secret
Pom Poko	The Social Dilemma
Red Dog	The Truman Show
Rush	The Way Way Back
Scent of a Woman	The Wind That Shakes the Barley
Serendipity	The Wolf of Wall Street
Seven Pounds	There Will Be Blood
Shawshank Redemption	Tik Tik Boom
Shutter Island	Trainspotting
Soul	Treasure Planet
Spirit	Unbroken
Spirited Away	What If
Spotlight	Where the Crawdads Sing
Stand By Me	Whiplash
Step Brothers	Yes Man
The Big Short	Zindagi Na Milegi Dobara

THE FUTURE

The Future encourages us to **Manifest**.

Manifest where you are heading. The final chapter covers disregarded threats and generational opportunities, fears of failure, bucket lists, future questions, potential futures, closing remarks at funerals and pieces of advice applicable to our future selves.

The following is the Student View of **The Future**.

What do you think is the most disregarded threat to our generation?

❖ Social Media and other forms of instant gratification. Our generation's neurochemistry and neurophysiology is being adjusted to a severe degree - at a rapid pace - and often in a negative direction.

❖ Confirmation Bias - People perceive basic facts in completely different ways biased to their own pre-existent world views. You can have two people in a room living completely irreconcilable realities because neither of them can accept basic facts that support the other side when it goes against their own beliefs. Algorithmic Bubbles on social media enable and magnify this issue.

❖ Housing Unaffordability.

❖ Societal judgement of coloured people.

❖ Disruptive innovation. Hear me out - conscious innovation is necessary and is what helps solve the world's problems, but innovation for the sake of constantly creating something new is creating a toxic society that is ungrateful for what it currently has. We have glorified newness and need to create new technologies to solve problems without creating a whole bunch more.

❖ The search for shortcuts. At work, at making food, at working out and seeking progress.

❖ Poor work ethic - people trying to make quick money and not putting in the hard work.

❖ We're not able to sit in silence. There was a day last year when Instagram, Facebook & WhatsApp had an outage. It was only for a period of about 24 hours, but people did not know what to do with themselves!

❖ The impact our over-dependence on technology and over-use of social media will have on people long-term.

❖ Self-optimising the whole time. It's okay not to stay up at 5 in the morning and run a half marathon and after that study for 12 hours.

❖ The metaverse.

❖ Wokeism.

❖ The increase in multitasking. It's really important to apply full focus on the current task at hand. Whether that's eating food, doing work, chatting to a friend, etc. you're able to truly 'live in the moment' when you're not thinking about anything else. There's so much anxiety & state of overwhelm in our current generation. We can learn this from older generations.

❖ Capitalism/ecological destruction.

❖ Mental health.

❖ The pursuit of infinite economic growth in a finite world.

❖ Cigarettes or drugs.

❖ I don't know if it's disregarded, but porn.

❖ Not reaching our potential due to the ease of having a sense of achievement. There is something for being hard on yourself.

❖ Inequality & women's rights.

❖ Mass automation of jobs.

❖ The pandemic really showed the lack of compassion people have with one another. I think if there ever comes a time humans are required to do something a little more than just wear a mask on their face to save the lives of others, we're all screwed.

❖ Insecurity.

❖ People thinking they are entitled to do whatever they want.

❖ I think the amount of online activity and work we do will negatively affect our ability to socialise with new people.

❖ Having too many options in all parts of our life and not being happy with the options we do take.

❖ A world run by increasingly stronger and bigger companies.

❖ Social media addiction. I know it is discussed a lot but I think we are all too okay with mindlessly scrolling on social media for hours and hours at a time, time that could be spent with family and friends, or practising hobbies, volunteering, reading etc. Not to mention the negative effects it has on our bodies (poor posture, eye strain) and brains (surely it can't be good to force our brains to consume information constantly for hours on end, day after day. Especially considering the sh*t on social media that we are forcing it to consume).

❖ Pressure that society puts on us. This pressure may stem from social media, family members, the government and more, where we have expectations to meet, which not everyone is destined for.

What do you think is the greatest opportunity for our generation?

❖ To travel. We have never been able to travel and work remotely as much as we can now. The more people that travel and learn about different cultures the better! Leads to less racism, narrow mindedness and helps people become better people! I think our generation should not worry so much about the future (e.g. getting a house, new car, new iPhone etc.) and spend their money on experiences. When you're on your deathbed you're not going to remember that new iPhone but you will remember the great experiences and people you met along the way!!

❖ To acknowledge the mistakes of the generation before us and strive to do better, for the generation that follows us. In all aspects of life - climate change, racism, etc.

❖ Escaping the 9-5.

❖ To overcome all of the negative impacts of technology and focus more on the benefits. Less excessive, individualistic thinking and more productive, collaborative innovation that isn't focused on instant gratification for oneself.

❖ To end violence against women.

❖ Inclusivity. The world we live in now is highly politicised in which people's choices in the way they live are questioned - this refers to gender, sexuality, identification and more. The greatest opportunity for our generation is to push a movement of "inclusiveness" in which people are able to live the life they desire to live without any hurt or shame coming their way. The world would be a better place if we were all more inclusive and accepting. :)

❖ The opportunity to meet people of different cultures and values and the merge of that.

❖ To realise that the reality that our parents grew up in is not necessarily the reality that you have to choose. We have so much information at our fingertips, so if you are not happy with your life's current direction, go find one which you are. Anything else would be a shame.

❖ Crypto and travelling.

❖ The greatest opportunity we have is to run for political office and integrate new ideas. In many places, older men still hold office, but our generation needs to be the ones to change that for good.

❖ Data Jobs - an open industry ready for anyone that is willing to put the time and effort in.

❖ Energy production.

❖ Essentially anything, everything is possible. It's a matter of doing at this point.

❖ We have the best technology available, we can do things in minutes which would take years. We have all the information we need on our phones, it's a very big blessing.

❖ The opportunity to work remotely.

❖ Quantum Computing.

❖ The greatest opportunity for our generation is the ability to change the world from the comfort of our own homes. While social media is perhaps one of the biggest threats, it can also be used to enact positive change in a way that no other generation was ever able to do.

❖ The freedom of information - not only can you find anything you could ever want but also share your own information. When used right this could change the world for the better.

❖ How creative we could be and how far we could move in technology.

❖ The internet. The ability to teach ourselves anything we can imagine, to work from anywhere in the world and the ability to interact with extremely wise and successful people is an absolute goldmine!

❖ Interconnected financial systems.

❖ Content creation and dissemination. Through ingenuity and hard work, it is now more feasible than ever before to make a living by monetising your passions, talents, and interests that are most meaningful to you.

❖ Access to information.

❖ Disrupting the widespread focus society has on normalising in slow motion and instead, focusing on embracing all quickly.

❖ To connect minds from all over the world to solve the most pressing global problems - via technology.

❖ A lot of us have access to new technology and resources, which we can better make a real difference in the world.

❖ We can influence more people using the internet/social media.

❖ The amount of knowledge at our fingertips that we are able to utilise at any point in time.

❖ The ease of travel! It's easier than ever to go somewhere.

❖ Tailoring new technology to our advantage.

❖ Networking! It's so easy to connect with other people and create meaningful relationships.

❖ Our generation has the great opportunity to redefine happiness and to seek out ways to enrich our lives beyond what we know. This is easier said than done because we live in very challenging times, but I believe adversity will only serve to benefit us, if only to strengthen our resolve to be better, do better and create the lives we want. Our greatest

Reflections   79

opportunity is to bring about a reset: one where WE define our own existence.

❖ To build sustainable, socially conscious businesses that seek to uplift while creating profit.

❖ The amount of information at our disposition.

❖ To put an end to capitalism, transition to a post-capitalistic system and preserve the environment and hundreds of thousands of lives.

❖ I think we have forgotten how to build meaningful relationships because of our online relationships with people and media. In college, we are given the freedom to begin shaping our own paths which can be entirely daunting. This can trigger a cascade of emotions that we haven't recognised before, or recognise again, or wish we didn't feel, but these emotions can produce emotional, exhilarating, petrifying, hilarious, fun, and happy moments that cultivate our own understanding of who we are and our perspective of the world. The opportunity to feel gratitude from providing ourselves with opportunities that are meaningful to us, the opportunities that we recognise as our own, are really powerful.

What will the world look like in 2032?

❖ The world will be a lot more seamless in 2032 and core values of compassion and value provision will uphold community creation. We will see a bridge between physical and digital assets and parallel economies being run on traditional and digital spectrums. The world will also see a shift in priorities for a lot of the youth from a money and ego driven society to a sustainability and unity driven environment overall.

❖ I think now more than ever I'm highly aware of how unpredictable the world is.

❖ Realistically, we won't be able to afford to live anywhere in Ireland, the cost of living will be astronomical, the impact on the climate will be irreversible. But hey, the new iPhone that year will probably be class.

❖ Very much the same but so very different; change will occur, but I am doubtful of revolutionary technological advances. The success or failure of late American capitalism will be clear. Polarisation will have increased along new and traditional lines and the debate on personal data protections will be or will have been settled one way or another. We will have created wonders, made money and experienced joy throughout. But I fear new wars and the new horrors they will bring.

❖ With the way things are advancing I am hoping that by then we'll have figured out a way to clean the oceans, slow down climate change, and have become a little more open and accepting towards people from all backgrounds. I like to stay optimistic.

❖ Climate change's consequences will be significant. I hope that we will be able to make our societies more sustainable, and become a more responsible global society.

❖ Exponentially more competitive than currently.

❖ A lot more technology present in every aspect of our life. Self-driving cars, a lot more electric cars. And unfortunately a world that is heavily dependent on media (social or other). Not a place I am looking forward to just yet.

❖ Overpopulated/congested.

❖ Underwater.

❖ Similar to now, but more involved in tech, going cashless, international travel made easier, hopefully climate change will be taken seriously.

❖ More people will begin to wake up to the realisation of the environment but it will be too late.

❖ Hotter, more tense and in political turmoil, frightened by an ever-growing outcry surrounding environmental, financial and political events.

❖ I have absolutely no idea which is both exciting and terrifying!

❖ Less money for the working class, higher cost of living and higher profits for corporations.

❖ Society will have revolted against cancel culture and free speech will be the number one ruler which will be as decisive as it is today.

❖ Hopefully a lot more green!!!

❖ Significantly different. Hard to predict, but I believe there will be even more pressure on the younger generations.

❖ Probably very bad, those in power are far too selfish.

❖ A world that is more environmentally conscious and in tune with nature.

❖ Better, although all we hear is negative news and stories, there are improvements happening everywhere.

❖ Without a major intervention, extremely polarised between left & right thinking thanks to algorithmic media. Globalisation & constant technological development will continue at a rapid pace in the developed world, with the developing world being left behind and creating a bigger gap between the rich & poor.

❖ Hopefully it's a good one where we've learned from the past and created a world where people enjoy life, have good balance between work, family, and social life.

❖ I think we've reached an inflection point in human history and large-scale changes will have to come about in a very short period of time to address the climate-change crisis. There could be a monumental global power-shift from West to East. I think 2032 will look very different from the present day.

What are your Top 3 Bucket List Items you would like to tick off before 2032?

1) Travel to Cape Horn, the most southerly point of the world before the South Pole **2)** Step foot in all EU states (18/27 completed) and all Balkan states (10/11 completed) **3)** Surf the Arctic swell

1) Start my own consulting business to help small suppliers break into large retailers **2)** Travel to as many countries as I can **3)** Be able to support my parents financially

1) Graduate with my Honours degree **2)** Get my driver's licence **3)** Learn to ride a bicycle

1) Read 200 books **2)** Hike Mount Batur in Bali **3)** Create an online portfolio

1) Raise my country count to 75 **2)** Build up more businesses and brands **3)** Have my skydive licence

1) Hitchhiking **2)** Skydiving **3)** Helping out small communities within Africa

1) Travel to South America **2)** Obtain a PhD **3)** Secure a job

1) Go to New York **2)** See Japanese cherry blossoms **3)** Skydive

1) Speak intermediately in at least 5 languages **2)** Do a triathlon **3)** Go skydiving

1) Jump out of an aeroplane **2)** Visit Japan **3)** Drive on 90-mile beach

1) Scuba diving **2)** Learn to play an instrument **3)** Travel as much as I can

1) Close an investment round **2)** Buy property **3)** Have moved to different companies

1) Skydive **2)** Travel Asia **3)** Tour the Outback

What are your Top 3 Bucket List Items you would like to tick off before 2032?

1) Play golf at Fancourt **2)** Go skydiving **3)** Learn to kiteboard

1) Work for a year in California **2)** Visit Brazil **3)** Attend an All Ireland hurling final

1) Climb Kilimanjaro **2)** Learn meditation 3) Travel Asia

1) Have been to each continent **2)** Run a marathon **3)** Complete college

1) Financial stability and independence **2)** Continuous authenticity **3)** To have whatever family situation I want :)

1) Become financially independent **2)** Launch a startup **3)** Ride a bike 300 km in a single day

1) Get married and have kids **2)** Write a suite of music **3)** Perform and teach music around the world

1) Travel **2)** Do something I've never done before, and could not even think of doing now **3)** Be fulfilled

1) Pass the bar **2)** Take a gap year **3)** Try as many sports as I can

1) Skydiving **2)** Shark cage diving **3)** Going to Tomorrowland

1) Work on the superyachts **2)** have an apartment in Germany or Netherlands **3)** Go on a nice holiday with a group of friends

1) Climb a giant mountain **2)** Learn to ski **3)** Read 10 books

1) Own restaurant **2)** Fly a plane **3)** Skydive

1) Backpacking trip through America's national parks in the Pacific Northwest **2)** Spend a year chasing the winter around the world and snowboarding **3)** Watch a Coldplay concert live

1) Renovate a self-sustaining home (energy/water/food) **2)** Visit every country in Europe overland **3)** Run a sub 2h30 marathon

1) Travel solo around my country of origin to reconnect and get a better understanding of my culture/roots **2)** Directly impact or help improve the lives of 100 people, that's 10 a year **3)** Start a business

What are you afraid of not achieving before 2032?

❖ Not finding something I am truly passionate about - something I am willing to sacrifice everything/die for.

❖ Fulfilling my potential, finding love, having an impact on life!

❖ I don't have any fear. What's for me won't go by me.

❖ I have stopped being afraid of what the future holds and started focusing on the present. I do have future goals but I don't worry about them too much.

❖ I'm cool with what I have, I would like a house but I'm ok if it doesn't happen.

❖ Not being able to buy my own property, not being able to take time out to go travelling for 6 months and not finding a job I genuinely am passionate about.

❖ Deciding exactly what I want to do with my life. It's a lot easier to score when you know where the goal is.

❖ This question is fundamentally wrong. Since fearing something at present encourages one to do so to avoid that future fear/ regret. So in that sense I should be afraid of things that I'm not afraid of now and they're unknown to me.

❖ Becoming a lawyer.

❖ Stability (in every way).

❖ Going to Australia and living my dream.

❖ Working in a job with a sense of purpose, where I am helping create a better, more balanced world even to a small degree, & not just earning to pay the bills.

❖ Writing my own novella or script.

❖ Being 30 and never having travelled the world.

❖ Having a house.

❖ Explore the world for the first few years, before beginning to settle down & start thinking about where my family & I may want to be.

❖ Have a stable job and travel around Europe.

❖ Finding a fulfilling purpose - everyone needs a purpose that drives them to either live to work, or to work to live.

❖ A stable relationship.

❖ Not earning and being as high up as I hope by that stage.

❖ Something that I can be truly proud of, regardless of what it may mean to others.

❖ I'm afraid of not taking enough risks. By 2032, I'll be in my 30's and presumably will have more responsibilities making it difficult to start a business or travel the world.

❖ Starting a political career.

❖ Financial and social leverage.

❖ Having a stable happy family & making my parents proud.

❖ I'm afraid of not having a job that makes me happy by 2032.

❖ Security and comfort.

❖ A wife.

❖ I'm afraid that I will give up chasing the dream and go back to having a boring life.

Meaningful Highlight 4
Who we see as an inspiring figure tells us what we value in a person.

Abbie Hoffman

Ailbhe Smyth

Alexandria Ocasio-Cortez

Amelia Earhart

Andrew Huberman

Barack Obama

Bayard Rustin

Bella Hadid

Bernie Sanders

Charles Feeney

Christopher Nolan

Dan Peña

Danny Devito

Dave

Dave Chapelle

David Goggins

David Norris

DBC Pierre

Dermot Earley

Donald Trump

Drake

Ed Mylett

Elon Musk

Emma Watson

Emmanuel Macron

Max Verstappen

Emmet Kirwan

F. Scott Fitzgerald

George Clooney

Greta Thunberg

J Cole

James Connolly

Jay Shetty

Joaquin Phoenix

Johnny Clegg

Jonah Hill

Jordan Peterson

Jürgen Klopp

Katie Taylor

Konrad Adenauer

Lenny Abrahamson

Leo Varadkar

Lionel Messi

Liz Bohannon

Malala Yousafzai

Marcus Rashford

Marie Curie

Mark Cuban

Martin Luthar King

Mary Oliver

Mary Robinson

Mesut Özil

Who we see as an inspiring figure tells us what we value in a person.

Michael Collins	Rosa Parks
Michael D. Higgins	Rosalía de Castro
Michael Jordan	Russell Brand
Michael B. Jordan	Ruth Bader Ginsburg
Michelle Obama	Sarah Blakely
Naval Ravikant	Sebastian Vettel
Neil deGrasse Tyson	Serena Williams
Nelson Mandela	Shakuntala Devi
Nims Dai	Sophie Turner
Nina Simone	Steve Biko
Oprah Winfrey	Steve Jobs
Oscar Wilde	Steven Gerrard
Patrick McAfee	Taylor Swift
Paul O'Donovan	Thich Nhat Hanh
Paula Scher	Tiger Woods
Paulo Coelho	Timothee Parrique
Pink	Trevor Noah
Princess Diana	Tyler Okonma
PV Sindhu	Tyson Fury
Rafael Nadal	Virat Kohli
Rafiki from the Lion King	Vitalik Buterin
Ray Dalio	Volodymyr Zelenskyy
Richard Feynman	Waris Dirie
Rihanna	Warren Buffet
Rob Williams	Wim Hof
Roger Federer	Zendaya
Rollie Peterkin	Does my mother count? Otherwise, I
Ronald Richman	don't have anyone
Ronaldo	

Who we see as an inspiring figure tells us what we value in a person.

Some contributors conveyed that their inspiration came from people closer to them, such as their family members & members of their community, while some stated that they are clearly not inspired by public figures at all.

If you could ask every student one question, what would you ask?

- ❖ "What do you do that makes you happy?" While happiness isn't necessarily something we can always strive for, feeling this emotion definitely gives our lives meaning. And vulnerability brings people closer together. I would be interested to see who would be able to answer this question with a real, raw and meaningful response.

- ❖ Would you rather be crying in a mansion or laughing in a slum?

- ❖ If you had the opportunity to do it all over again without changing a thing, would you?

- ❖ What would you study if money was irrelevant?

- ❖ What is something you can tell me that would be of benefit?

- ❖ What mark do you want to leave in your community?

- ❖ Do you think you study too much, at the compromise of fun and living your life? If yes/no, do you think you'll regret it in 20+ years when you look back?

- ❖ Do you think you have found what you are best at, and if so, is that what you are pursuing?

- ❖ Are you happy with your current life direction?

- ❖ What is your dream?

- ❖ You get to wish for one thing for the campus. What would that be?

- ❖ Where do you think will you be happy? "Where" could be interpreted as what company/role, city/country, circumstances, with whom around.

❖ What is a passion that you haven't truly fulfilled yet? When do you plan to?

❖ I just see people chasing a secure job rather than their personal satisfaction, but I guess that is just the way it works in Business, and I partially see myself falling into this temptation too. But despite that, I see myself well able to answer this question (can tell you all the circumstances that'd make me happy?). I wonder if anyone can answer it as easily.

❖ What was your most wholesome moment in life?

❖ Why are you studying and what you are studying?

❖ Do you believe we're put on here to find meaning or to experience as much as possible?

❖ What do you wish your professor did differently?

❖ What will you regret the most when you're lying on your deathbed?

❖ If for some reason you weren't able to attend college, what would you have done?

❖ Are you happy with your degree or would you rather be doing something else?

❖ What are your ambitions?

❖ What blows your mind?

❖ What aspect of your personality has changed the most during your time at college?

❖ What is holding you back?

❖ What will you miss most upon graduation?

❖ What's the funniest thing that you've seen or experienced in college life?

If you could ask every student one question, what would you ask?

- ❖ Why did you pick your course?

- ❖ What do you think happens to us when we die?

- ❖ Which interest outside of the scope of your college course has been most beneficial to you?

- ❖ What is the goal of your future career?

- ❖ What are you gaining from your time in university?

- ❖ Where do swallows go at night?

- ❖ Do you genuinely enjoy going out and drinking?

- ❖ What motivates you?

- ❖ What makes you smile?

- ❖ Reflect on one of the most painful experiences of your life. Did the painful experience lead to progress?

- ❖ Do you think our primitive brain is capable of surviving in this modern world?

What's a statement you would like someone to say about you at your funeral?

❖ You achieved your purpose.

❖ She always kept her promises and made people smile everywhere she went. She also fought a bear and won.

❖ He could entertain people through his hilarious jokes, enthralling stories & songs of passion.

❖ He worked harder than you could ever imagine and did some incredible things.

❖ That I came a long way despite difficulties and challenges because of my strength and resilience, and that I was always a good friend to those around me.

❖ She would have laughed if she were here.

❖ He spoke about his emotions & didn't let ego get in his way.

❖ I would like people to recognise how much time and effort I gave into helping others.

❖ She taught me more than she thought. She inspired me to become a better person for myself, not for others.

❖ He lived and he learned.

❖ He was a real gentleman.

❖ She knew who she was.

❖ He treated everyone with the same amount of respect.

❖ I'd like people to all symbiotically agree with who I was, then I would know I was transparent. That I was my true self to whoever I was with.

❖ A guy you couldn't help but love, with a smile that would take centre stage in a room full of people.

❖ She didn't take no for an answer.

❖ I was a compassionate soul who was not afraid to accept challenges and explore new horizons.

❖ That I never stopped living with compassion.

❖ Above all, I would like to be remembered as a kind individual who brought happiness to others. I also hope that, when others reflect on my life one day, that it is a full and authentic one.

❖ She stood up for herself & for what was right.

❖ He's still living, in our memories, our hearts & the way we see life.

❖ He always made me laugh.

❖ That he stayed committed to his goals and made people know how much he cared about them and that he could always be counted on, even in the most trying times.

❖ One of a kind.

❖ That my intentions were always clear & I was a genuine person.

❖ A woman who never stopped trying to improve herself & the lives around her.

❖ That I am a moral yet loyal friend.

❖ She knew what her gift was & used it to her fullest potential.

❖ I've never met anyone like her.

What's a statement you would like someone to say about you at your funeral?

❖ He never took people for granted.

❖ He encouraged me to flourish as a Human.

❖ Worked hard, stayed true to what he believed in and stayed loyal to those he loved.

❖ She had a lot of fun.

❖ He always went whatever direction he wanted to go at that point in time and that way of thinking brought him all around the world and experienced everything.

❖ That I never stopped loving, exploring & appreciating the human experience. Death is inevitable. Love living!

What is the best advice you have ever received?

❖ "You actually have to speak to girls to get a girlfriend."

❖ I once watched a video on stoicism and there was a quote from it saying, "You can't control what happens to you, but you can control how you react to it." Ever since adopting this philosophy, I feel a heightened level of maturity, and feel more secure in conversing with people. Pausing upon someone saying something and then reflecting on it in a genuine way before reacting has helped me a lot.

❖ "We regret the risks we failed to take. Take them."

❖ "Be among the believers and do work that is of service to you and society."

❖ "It is what it is. Do not try to control that which you cannot. Accept the inevitable and recognise that we are part of a greater whole, that which we simply cannot even begin to comprehend, but can acknowledge after experiencing the ups and downs and the beautiful lessons that accompany them, embodying the human experience."

❖ "Before you do something, ask yourself why."

❖ "Everyone has started from the beginning."

❖ "As long as you do your best, then you should never beat yourself up for something that is out of your control. You did your best and therefore the only way forward is to take whatever you can learn from it and try to improve for next time. Always move forward."

❖ "You will pay tomorrow for what you did not do today."

❖ "Take your earphones out and look around."

❖ "To breathe."

❖ "To love others intentionally and live everyday like it's my last."

❖ "Love is like a fart. If you force it, it's sh*t."

❖ "When you are stuck on making a decision, do what is right and not what is easy. The journey is more important than the result."

❖ "Take a few steps back and look at the situation from a distance."

❖ "Take it step by step, don't stress."

Applies to any time I feel overwhelmed about assignments, the uncertainty about next year, the time that is left before my next travel plans or before seeing loved ones.

❖ "Focus on the present, everything happens for a reason (it doesn't take away pain but makes you move on with your life and not dwell on the past.)"

❖ "Picture yourself on your deathbed, right before your last breath…

What advice do you think you would give yourself right now? Whatever it is, do that, as of this moment."

❖ "Do everything in moderation - even including moderation."

❖ "Everyone has imposter syndrome—not just you. Welcome to being an adult."

❖ "Never stop your quest for finding yourself."

❖ "You can't truly know how to rest if you don't know how to work."

❖ "The quest for certainty blocks the search for meeting."

❖ "Don't put things off to a later date."

❖ "My worst ever moment as a parent was walking into the living room and seeing you sitting next to your grandmother, playing on your iPad. Who knows how many more years she has, talk to her."

I always refer back to this moment. In an age where man is becoming like machine & machine is becoming like man, we need to make sure we don't forget what keeps us human. If we don't maintain our emotional intelligence capabilities, we are no longer human.

❖ "Don't make promises you can't keep."

❖ "Trust yourself, you're so much stronger and smarter than you realise."

❖ "You find meaning through hardship."

❖ "Always be in search of your next challenge."

❖ "What if it turns out better than you expected?"

❖ "The world is made to be free in. Give up all other worlds except the one in which you belong."

❖ "Help as many people as you can."

❖ "Do then feel. Don't feel then do."

❖ 1. "What's (honestly) the worst that could happen?"

2. "It's not about the journey or the destination but the company you have with you."

❖ "Always ask for help when you need it." This could be emotional help, help with work/school, help with a new skill! Anything! Use the support structures and resources available to you.

❖ "Memento mori" - remember that you have to die.

❖ "Carpe diem". We don't know how much longer we'll be here for. Seize the day!

Manifest

The Japanese word for crisis - 危機 ('Kiki') contains two characters. The first meaning 'dangerous' and the second meaning 'opportunity'. Leading into the year 2032, we saw contributors describe their anxieties about the direction the world is heading on a collective level, particularly technologically & environmentally. Simultaneously, some see this danger as an opportunity, with possibilities to benefit from living in a connected, globalised world. While on a collective level, we often have little influence. On an individual level, everyone has grand plans and dreams they hope to experience before they die. The Bucket Lists we saw, in particular, exemplify a sense of adventure and desire. How many of these desires will be actualised? Do we enjoy dreaming more than we enjoy achieving? Many can give others brilliant advice but are not able to live by this advice themselves. We are all brilliant philosophers, therapists & teachers until it comes to being inside our own heads. We should be listening to the pieces of advice we offer more than anyone else. Perhaps we will regret not listening more to our advice when we look back. Focus on your actions as an individual, listen to yourself in anticipation, and bring your and others' ideal future to life.

Manifest where you are heading.

Where We Were. Where We Are. Where We're Heading.

Reflections tell us where we were, where we are and where we're heading. With 45 nationalities represented, we've acknowledged the reflections of over 100 individuals. To conclude, we think it would be helpful to share our perspective and the perspective of those who contributed regarding the experience of creating the book.

Our perspective as authors begins with our whys. We'd think the whys provide insight into our motives. You can find some of our whys below:

- ❖ *To understand that everyone in life has a different perspective.*
- ❖ *To encourage the use of hindsight and reflection to make a change in your present, with the hope that it will improve your future.*
- ❖ *To build meaningful relationships and do meaningful work.*
- ❖ *To test whether you can achieve things when you chuck yourself out there, and by asking! The Law of Attraction and Manifestation applied.*
- ❖ *To test whether an idea early in your late teens/early 20s can change the course of your life.*

Secondly, we'd like to comment on the perspective of those who contributed. A resounding number of contributors mentioned how much the questions made them think! From our perspective, your contributions have made us realise that it can be helpful to step away from the noisy world and instead spend time reflecting on oneself. One could argue that our generation finds it difficult to reflect. Often reflection is only encouraged in specific environments, such as therapy or within the context of very close relationships. As authors, we don't claim to know everything. We can only try our best to follow many of the positive messages presented in this book and hope the book contributes toward positive change.

Throughout the book, we've investigated psychological fires. Imprints & experiences that encourage us to grow. Contributors shared their meaningful memories, hopes and fears, pains and gains without the fear of unreasonable judgement and close-mindedness. Powered by this approach, we hope you, the reader, will embrace the reflections, using collective hindsight for foresight. **We hope that we have outlined the importance of reflecting. The fires are inevitable, but our ability to control them and grow from them is manageable. Our journey in putting this book together and taking in the different perspectives has enhanced our own perceptions. And we hope the different perspectives have enhanced your own perception too.**

The Authors of Reflections: The Student View

You can find more information about us on the following page in the form of three bios. We hope each bio gives a bit of insight into each of us and outlines where we were, where we are and where we're heading. If you are interested in reaching out to our team, feel free to contact us via our points of contact:

Email: Comms.Reflections@gmail.com

Instagram: @ReflectionsMedia_ig

LinkedIn: ReflectionsMedia

About Callum

Hey! I'm Callum. I was born in London to a British mother and an Irish father. I moved to Ireland when I was six. I still have vivid memories of leaving the UK, abruptly saying goodbye to my best friend, and knowing a different childhood awaited me in Dublin, Ireland. I was welcomed openly to Portmarnock despite my English accent and enjoyed making friends with a diverse set of kids while playing football as much as possible. During secondary school, I formed a friendship with Ravi. We had meaningful discussions at the back of the bus heading home from school, realising we were like-minded but also very different. We met Johnny during our final year of university in late 2021. It was a similar experience to when Ravi and I met. Like-minded but so different. Which I think brought us closer together!

I graduated with a degree in Commerce from University College Dublin with a focus on finance. But I love a broad learning experience. I live for learning, especially concerning humanity, which was a central motivation for this project. I primarily learn by reading, with a strong interest in psychology and general cause-and-effect relationships. Despite the importance of building a career, I'm excited to travel now. To meet different people hitchhiking with Johnny across Central Asia and embrace an expedition to India, where I aim to complete a two-week trek with my Auntie and Uncle. I've got a personal goal to improve my understanding of the world, its people and myself. This book has helped me move closer to achieving my aim but, more importantly, I hope it helps others achieve their goals too.

Callum's Personal Reflection: Speak less, execute more.

About Ravi

Hey there! My name is Ravi. I was born in Ireland to a family of 1st generation immigrants from India. While there are historical similarities with both countries, they have 2 very contrasting cultures. As a result, when I was in India, I was too Irish to be Indian, and when I was in Ireland, I was too Indian to be Irish. A tale I'm sure many children of immigrant families can relate to. Being exposed to both cultures growing up was confusing at times, but in hindsight, one of the best things that could've happened to me. I realised the value of standing out from the crowd and fully embraced it in all facets of my life. As Callum mentioned, we met in secondary school and we'd talk about all sorts of topics on the bus back from school. However, something we were always quite aware of was the fact that we were no experts in the stuff we were talking about, and were probably wrong.

When I joined university to study Computer Science, I was in the mindset of trying to get to know as many people as I possibly could. As a result, I came across some really fascinating individuals. I met aspiring entrepreneurs, actors, politicians, athletes and many more. Johnny was one of these people that I met, an individual who strives to make positive change in the world. Callum, Johnny and I would engage in some really interesting discussions and debates. We all have very different perspectives of the world, and that's what made it so interesting. As for my future, I plan to break out of my comfort zone and take opportunities that enable me to do work on challenging, yet impactful work.

Ravi's Personal Reflection: One conversation can change your life, speak to people.

About Johnny

Hiya, I'm Johnny. I was born in Ireland but grew up in South Africa where I moved with my family when I was 5. I'm extremely grateful for growing up in a loving, wacky & transparent family who I've developed a lot of my core values from. My Hungarian mum, Irish dad & 2 younger sisters all live back in Cape Town, where I used to be known as the Irish guy. Since moving back to Ireland, I have experienced a bit of an identity crisis as I've been referred to as the South African guy! I feel lucky to have this multicultural background and am proud of these 3 nationalities in me, but I've come to the realisation that I'm Johnny before anything else, & am conscious of labelling anyone by where they are from. Where we come from shouldn't define us (:

Right now, I live for smiles & travelling. I absolutely love meeting people & diving into deep, meaningful conversations. From the get-go, Callum, Ravi & I dove into these types of conversations, forming a strong connection despite our differences. I'm all for achieving a certain level of discomfort in order to grow & aim to do this consistently. Hitchhiking has taught me valuable lessons about humanity, hospitality & overcoming the fear of uncertainty. I've just graduated from a Bachelor of Commerce Degree with Spanish in the University College of Dublin. Career wise, I strive to use my business knowledge & interpersonal skills to create a meaningful impact & narrow inequality gaps. In this very exciting, but somewhat overwhelming, phase of life after college, my plan is to travel for the next year around Central Asia (initially with Callum), followed by South America in 2023. I cannot wait to continue learning, explore worlds I don't know & keep progressing in my personal development.

Johnny's Personal Reflection: Seek discomfort - that's when you reach a level of growth. First Year was more about being as comfortable as possible, now I strive to become comfortable with the uncomfortable.

From this experience, we have gained value from Reflections. Although contemplating positive and negative experiences can be uncomfortable, we believe contemplation has enhanced our growth. We strive to continue to learn from our own perspectives and those of others. We encourage you to do the same and use a notebook to record your own reflections.

Community is important to us. This book is a starting point. Our vision for the future is to encourage Reflections to learn more about ourselves and others.

If you've made it this far, scan the QR code below to answer the 25 questions featured in this book!

Printed in Great Britain
by Amazon

85132174R00072